HEALTHY RECIPES & MEAL PLANNERS TO HELP YOU...

EAT SHOP SAVE

DALE PINNOCK

hamlyn

An Hachette UK Company
www.hachette.co.uk

First published in Great Britain in 2018 by Hamlyn,
an imprint of Octopus Publishing Group Ltd
Carmelite House
50 Victoria Embankment
London EC4Y 0DZ
www.octopusbooks.co.uk

ISBN 978 1 78472 534 1

A CIP catalogue record for this book is available from the British Library.

Printed and bound in Italy

13 5 7 9 10 8 6 4 2

Editorial Director: Eleanor Maxfield
Editor: Sophie Elletson
Assistant Editor: Nell Warner
Design and Art Direction: Smith & Gilmour Ltd

CONTENTS

INTRODUCTION

Here in the UK we seem to have got into a little bit of trouble. Our health is declining at an alarming rate. Over 60 per cent of people in the UK are now classed as overweight or obese. There are over 3 million of us with diabetes, almost 90 per cent of which have type 2 diabetes which, in all but a few cases, is caused by lifestyle. Coronary artery disease will kill one in six men, and one in ten women. There are nearly 200,000 heart attacks in the UK each year, and 2.3 million people living with cardiovascular disease. The thing is, these diseases are not due to bad genes or hard luck; in all but a tiny percentage they are because of the way that we live. It is as simple as that.

Now, don't get me wrong, I am not wagging the finger of blame and claiming you should know better. Our modern way of living is skewed. We live in a world where time is a precious commodity. Our funds don't stretch as far as they used to as salaries haven't moved in accordance with inflation. Supermarkets take advantage of this to sell processed ready meals that save us time and save us money – but if they make us sick, what is the point? The basics of nutrition are not taught in schools. Newspapers and magazines are filled to the brim with fad diets, conflicting advice and sensationalist headlines. Put this all together and we have an environment in which making good health choices becomes a precarious minefield. So, yes, these health issues are linked to the way we live, but they are not our FAULT. We just need guidance on how to navigate this modern way of living that presents so many challenges.

That is what we set out to do with the *Eat, Shop, Save* series on ITV, and it's what I want to really cement in this book. On the television programme, a team of experts help four families rise to the *Eat, Shop, Save* challenge with amazing success. All the participants save money, lose weight, become savvier shoppers, learn to cook healthy, fresh food and run more efficient households. As a result of these small but significant lifestyle changes, all family members feel happier, healthier and wealthier and spend more quality time together. Now it's your turn to give it a go with this cookbook packed full of tips. I want to show you that with a little bit of know-how, a fresh perspective and some practical ideas, you can be healthier, you can feel better and you can save some money.

DALE PINNOCK

SAVE £ TIME

One of the biggest hurdles that we found when making the series, and also that I have found with my own private clients, is a lack of time. Let's face it, our modern lives are pretty bonkers. Our schedules are becoming ever more full. We often have unusual working hours, different shifts, within families parents can have different working patterns, children are at different schools and have different hobbies and extracurricular activities. All of this means that, for many of us, time is a scarce commodity, and sadly this seems to take its toll on the one area of our life we need to pay the most attention to in such crazy times – our own wellbeing. With such pressures, many people fall into the convenience trap. The frozen ready meals. The takeaways. Now, I'm not saying either of these are inherently bad in the slightest. I love the odd takeaway. But a diet that is built predominantly on these things, over fresh foods, can create problems in the long term. We all know they can. These foods tend to have significantly higher levels of trans fats, sugar and refined salt. They are also often very depleted in micronutrients – those all-important vitamins and minerals.

So how do we eat well and look after our health when we are time poor? Well, thankfully I have a few tricks up my sleeve to tackle this very issue.

BATCH COOKING

This is something that I mentioned repeatedly during the series. Batch cooking is the number one hack for people that are pushed for time but are committed to eating better. It is a super easy way to get ahead and save time, and most definitely save money.

I believe that, no matter what, we can always find time. Always. If there is one day a week where you can find an extra hour or two, say a Sunday afternoon, use this time to cook. With batch cooking, you simply cook up your favourites but increase the amount – three to four times more than you would normally cook. You then freeze this in individual portions. You can get single-portion takeaway-style containers that fit snuggly in the freezer. Then, after a long day, you simply take these dishes out of the freezer, defrost and voila! A healthy home-cooked meal. No extra spending, no nasties, and you can make it exactly how you like it.

 Dishes such as curries, chillies, stews and soups are all perfect for batch cooking, and you will find plenty of inspiration throughout the book. To make it even easier, these recipes are marked with a handy symbol.

MEAL PREPPING

Pre-preparing food is something that is becoming very popular of late, and rightfully so. Just look on Instagram and you will see hundreds of pictures of lunch boxes lined up and filled with healthy food for the week.

You don't have to get completely obsessive over this, but a little bit of preparation can save you time. It's pretty simple. For example, in the book we have recipes for snacks, such as dips and spreads, which also make great sandwich fillers.

You can make your workday lunches ahead of time too. So many of the people I work with find that their lunch is one of the things that lets them down. Many don't even stop for lunch as they feel that they don't have time to go to the shops or even make the trip to the staff canteen. Or for some the workplace can be an absolute den of sins, with cakes and chocolate, or endless supplies of chips in the canteen. Prepping your workday lunch ticks all the boxes – it saves you time, saves you money, and saves you from bad choices. We have some great ideas for make-ahead lunches in the recipes chapters later on.

FROZEN FRUIT AND VEGETABLES TO LOOK OUT FOR:

PEAS	BLACKBERRIES
SPINACH	STRAWBERRIES
BROCCOLI	MANGO
BLUEBERRIES	PINEAPPLE
RASPBERRIES	

PRE-PREPARED FRIDGE AND FREEZER STAPLES

This is the final time-saving hack. It is always a good idea to stock up on frozen fruit and vegetables. There is the strange idea that frozen produce isn't as nutritious as 'fresh'. Nothing could be further from the truth. Most frozen produce is frozen within hours of getting picked. Many of the important nutrients, vitamin C for example, begin to reduce in number immediately after the produce has been picked. The longer the produce is left after picking, the more the nutrient content can decline. Much of the 'fresh' fruit and veg that you see on the shelves may have actually been harvested a month to six weeks ago, and left in cold storage before being taken out to order. This affects the micronutrient density considerably. Frozen varieties have more of the vitamins intact, and most are pre-prepared so you need to do very little in the way of peeling or chopping. You can just get straight on with the cooking. They are often cheaper too!

In the fridge I almost always have pre-chopped fresh vegetables on hand for days when I just want to dip in and grab something with minimal fuss. Of course pre-cooked meats are great, and you can now even get things like pre-peeled avocados or pre-hardboiled eggs. Be aware, though, that we often pay for convenience!

SAVE YOUR HEALTH

This is really where the rubber hits the road. It's where things get serious. As we have seen, the nation's health is in real trouble, and there is no escaping the fact that our diet is one of the fundamental key areas that can influence this positively and negatively. The problem many of us have, funds and time aside, is a clear idea of what eating healthily actually IS. The modern press is obsessed with nutrition, and social media is absolutely on fire with it. This has led to such distorted facts, fads, myths and mayhem, that for most people, they just don't know where to start. However, to those of us that have studied the subject and follow the evidence, the story is pretty clear and we can guide you to how to set yourself up with better eating habits for life. It isn't complicated, it isn't hard, it isn't costly. It is as simple as you can get.

KNOW YOUR FATS

If there is one area of nutrition that is massively misunderstood and also feared, it is fat in the diet. This is something you NEED to know about as getting it wrong can seriously damage your health. Again, though, the beauty is that the practicalities are very simple.

For decades we have been told to avoid saturated fat like the plague, and instead opt for the 'heart healthy' vegetable oils. In that time so many of us switched over to oils like sunflower oil, corn oil, soya bean oil or regular vegetable oil. We also ditched butter and opted for margarine instead. So, while these oils are not saturated fats, the move has caused major problems, and it is all to do with substances in the oils called 'essential fatty acids'.

There are a few fatty acids but the big two are called omega 3 and omega 6. You may have heard of these. They are vitamin-like substances that have some vital roles to play in the body, from building structures in the eyes and the brain through to regulating some important biochemical events in our body, one of the main events being inflammation.

Now, when it comes to inflammation, they act differently. These fatty acids get converted by the body into substances called prostaglandins, whose job it is to regulate inflammation. Some prostaglandins switch inflammation on and accelerate it, and some switch it off and tone it down. There are three types of prostaglandin – Series 1, Series 2 and Series 3. Series 1 and Series 3 switch off and reduce inflammation. Series 2 switch inflammation on. Ok…take a breather.

Now, the different fatty acids get turned into different prostaglandins. Omega-3 fatty acids get converted into the anti-inflammatory Series 1 and Series 3 prostaglandins. Omega-6 fatty acids on the other hand get converted into the Series 2 prostaglandins that switch on and worsen inflammation.

So, what has any of this got to do with the fats and oils we choose? Well, oils such as vegetable oil, sunflower oil, soya bean oil, corn oil and margarines are incredibly rich in omega-6 fatty acids. If your omega 6 intake is too high, and you are not taking in enough omega 3 from foods such as oily fish (salmon, mackerel and sardines, for example), then we feed the chemical pathways that switch on inflammation in the body. If this happens long term then we can cause considerable damage to the heart and circulatory system, worsen inflammatory issues such as joint pain and skin flare-ups, and put ourself at risk of many serious diseases.

So what do we do? It's time to ditch those oils. If you have any of these oils or margarines in your cupboards and fridge, bundle them all together and throw them in the bin, and never look back. From now on, for cooking use almost exclusively olive oil. This is because the most dominant fatty acid in olive oil is one called omega 9, which has no influence on inflammation. By making this simple swap alone you are cutting out vast amounts of omega 6. In place of margarine, it is butter all the way, just don't eat a pack a day!

Finally, and something I advise everyone to do, is to increase your intake of omega-3 fatty acids. This helps to protect you against excessive inflammation, not to mention delivering a myriad of other health benefits for the heart, brain, eyes and immune system.

FATS: THE GOOD AND THE BAD

TO EAT	TO AVOID
SALMON	SUNFLOWER OIL
MACKEREL	CORN OIL
SARDINES	VEGETABLE OIL
NUTS E.G. WALNUTS	SOYA BEAN OIL
SEEDS E.G. CHIA AND FLAXSEEDS	MARGARINE
OLIVE OIL	
BUTTER (IN MODERATION)	

GET CARB SMART

Carbohydrates have got a lot of flack in the media in recent years, and to a great degree I feel this is justified. Too much of the wrong ones and you are in trouble. It all has to do with the effect your carbohydrate intake has on your blood sugar levels.

Blood sugar is, as the name suggests, the amount of sugar that we have in our bloodstream that can be shipped to our cells for them to make into energy. Blood sugar levels have to be within a very specific range. Too much or too little is a problem. When we eat, the glucose in our food enters our bloodstream. The body responds to this by releasing the hormone insulin, which tells our cells that glucose is available to use for energy. When cells receive this signal, they open their doors and take in the glucose. This is what happens when things are working normally. The problem occurs when we have too much sugar in our bloodstream. When this happens, we release insulin, and the cells begin to take up glucose. However, cells have a cut-off point. They can only take in a certain amount of sugar before they get full, as too much can cause major damage to the cell. And so they shut their doors. If this pattern is happening every day, our cells become resistant to insulin, and eventually we can go on to develop type 2 diabetes where we are not able to control our blood sugar levels properly.

When our blood sugar is high, the excess gets sent off to our liver where it turns into something we can store – a type of fat. This fat leaves the liver and gets sent to our fat tissue. We put on weight. Furthermore, this fat is transported to our fat tissue via our circulation, so the fats in our blood go up drastically, causing an increased risk of heart disease.

So what causes this type of high blood sugar? It is the type of carbohydrates we eat that is the problem. In general, we are consuming way too much of the wrong types of carbohydrates. Foods such as white bread, white rice, white pasta, processed sugars, sweets, chocolate and fizzy drinks all contain very high levels of simple carbohydrates that are rapidly released into the bloodstream. However, it's also the amount of carbohydrate that we eat that exacerbates the issue. Let's use this example: how many people would opt for some cereal and a slice of toast for breakfast, a sandwich and a packet of crisps for lunch and then some pasta or mashed potatoes in the evening? This isn't unusual. It is actually very typical of the eating habits of a lot of people. Now, not all these foods are necessarily 'bad'. I am not vilifying anything. But the pattern and the level of consumption is the issue. A consistent amount of simple carbohydrates will push blood sugar levels up so far that, over weeks, months and years we can pile on weight, and increase our risk of diabetes and heart disease.

So what should we do instead? I tell people to be carb smart, which consists of two things. The first is the choice of carbohydrates that you consume. Ditch the white bread, white rice, white pasta and swap over to the brown. Like bread? Simply opt for a multigrain instead of white. Pasta? Go for wholewheat. Swap your white rice for brown rice. It's that simple. What makes the brown varieties better? Its all about the fibre. These high-fibre versions take longer to digest, which means it takes longer for them to release their energy; their sugars enter the bloodstream as a gentle trickle rather than a massive flood, keeping blood sugar at a level that our cells can deal with without any of the issues mentioned above. The other benefit of fibre is that it keeps your digestive system working like clockwork – you know what I mean! Plus, these versions of your carbohydrate staples are much higher in vitamins and minerals.

A WORD ON CALORIES

Being aware of the calorie content of your meals can also be a helpful way to know if you are eating the right amount of food. As well as following a healthy, balanced diet, your calorie intake should be around 2,500 for men and 2,000 for women to maintain your current weight. This number will vary, however, depending on age, lifestyle, weight, etc. Vegetables, fruit, pulses and wholegrains are often naturally low in calories, whereas dairy products, oils, nuts and seeds (i.e. foods with a higher fat content) are often naturally high in calories and should be consumed in moderation. There are some brilliant apps and websites to help you, such as the NHS calorie checker.

GET PORTION-SIZE SAVVY

Another part of getting carb smart is the amount that you eat. At mealtimes, a quarter of your plate should be taken up by your wholegrain carbohydrates or low-glycaemic starchy vegetables such as sweet potatoes. Another quarter of the plate should contain your protein (meat, fish, eggs, tofu, beans, etc). The remaining half of the plate should be made up of non-starchy vegetables – especially the green leafy variety.

One of the best ways to keep your weight in check and get healthier is to get portion-size savvy. Even if you are eating more nutritious foods, it won't pay off unless you are eating the right quantities! When it comes to carbs, always read the packaging as it can tell you how much a portion size is. Here is a handy guide to help:

RICE = 50–70g (uncooked weight) per person (around a handful)

PASTA = up to 75g (uncooked weight) per person (around two handfuls)

BREAD = 1 or 2 slices per person

CEREAL = 40g per person (around 6 tablespoons)

AIM FOR YOUR PLATE TO LOOK SOMETHING LIKE THIS:

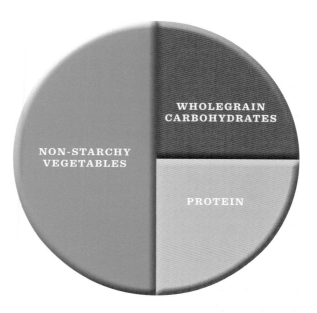

COLOUR UP YOUR PLATE

One of the best ways that you can give your diet a healthy upgrade is by making it as colourful as possible. So many of us can go for days or even weeks without any kind of fresh food passing our lips. Brightly coloured fresh fruit and vegetables are packed to the hilt with vitamins, minerals, antioxidants and phytochemicals (chemicals in plants that aren't nutrients per se, but can delivery a pharmacological effect). Different colours will represent different spectrums of nutrients and antioxidants. This is why it is important to get as many different colours into your diet as possible. It gives you a broad intake of all the good stuff.

GIVE YOUR FAVOURITES A FACELIFT

One of the biggest hurdles to eating healthier is actually getting started! For many the idea of giving up their favourite food and living on salads and broccoli for the rest of their life fills them with dread and makes them not want to bother. Totally understandable. If I thought that's what my diet was going to be for the rest of my life, I wouldn't bother either. But who on earth said it had to be this way? Why would you want to give up the food you love?

If you want to eat healthier and make new habits stick, then the place to start is to give your favourites a facelift! Learn how to take your favourite meal and make a healthier version of it. You like pizza? Why not make a base using a wholemeal bread mix and top it with vegetables like roasted veg and then some goat's cheese. You like spaghetti bolognese? Awesome, throw a few cooked lentils into the sauce to up the fibre, and swap the spaghetti for the wholewheat version. You get the picture. Start by learning how to take your favourite meals, the stuff you already love to eat, and make them better. Luckily we have a whole chapter of recipes dedicated to just that.

VEGETARIAN AND VEGAN

In recent years we have seen a huge rise in vegetarianism and veganism. There are many things that have spurred this trend, from celebrity endorsements through to documentaries and published research hitting the headlines. Some adopt this diet and lifestyle from an ethical standpoint, driven by animal rights and environmental issues. Others adopt it as a step towards better health, and this is where things need a little clarity. Take this from someone who was vegan for twenty years (I'm not now) – issues can crop up so being prepared for them and taking the right steps can keep you on track.

Generally speaking, vegetarian and vegan diets do tend to be a lot healthier than the average UK diet. They tend to contain more dietary fibre, more fruits and vegetables (although I do know vegans that live on chips and soy burgers ... not exactly a fast track to health by any means) and more wholegrains. However, you do need to be aware that you can become deficient in certain nutrients if you're not careful, but these can easily be found in supplements.

OMEGA-3 FATTY ACIDS

These are vitamin-like substances found in certain oily foods that have a vital role to play in the body. They are involved in maintaining structures in the eyes and in the brain. They also play a role in regulating inflammation in the body, as well as keeping the heart healthy and supporting the immune system. The problem is that in plants, omega 3 appears in the ALA form that the body has to convert to EPA and DHA before it can be used. This is a relatively inefficient process. Animal foods such as oily fish, however, already contain EPA and DHA and are therefore a more efficient source. Upping your intake of chia seeds, flaxseeds and walnuts as well as taking an EPA/DHA supplement derived from algae will tick the box.

VITAMIN B12

Vitamin B12 is a nutrient that has a key role to play in the normal functioning of the brain and the nervous system. It is also vital for the formation of red blood cells. B12 is only found in animal-derived products or supplements. A deficiency in this nutrient can in the short term produce symptoms such as fatigue, breathlessness, poor memory and pale skin. The more serious effects arise when intake of B12 has been low for a long time. Long-term B12 deficiency can lead to mania and psychosis, as well as increased risk of cardiovascular disease. A good daily vitamin B complex will keep you out of the woods here.

IRON

The final nutrient to be aware of is iron. This can easily become deficient with a vegan diet, but is usually OK with a vegetarian diet. There are plant forms of iron which go some way to keep our iron levels in check (plant-based sources include beans, pulses and green leafy veg), but they are a poor second to the 'haem iron' found in animal products, which is more easily absorbed. Therefore, vegetarians and vegans can have an elevated risk of anaemia, which can result in fatigue, breathlessness, dizziness and pale skin. Add a daily multivitamin and mineral to cover your bases.

All in all, vegetarian and vegan diets are very healthy when, like the bulk of the food in this book, they are built around whole foods with loads of fresh ingredients. Keep the above in mind and you won't go far wrong.

SAVE MONEY

There is a belief among many that eating healthily is an expensive pursuit. Sure, you can very easily spend a lot of money if you choose weird faddy ingredients or go to the high-end supermarkets. But eating healthily isn't all grass-fed unicorn and biodynamic dino-broccoli grown by a wizard in Salisbury. Of course, there is that side to the health world, but it is one that I detest and one that really isn't of relevance to 99 per cent of us. Eating healthily, as you will see in the following chapters, is really just about getting back to basics, using good ingredients, being aware of how we cook things and learning what makes good choices. And that's it. It doesn't have to be laborious, expensive, bland and boring, or anything else of the sort.

KNOW YOUR LOCAL OUTLETS

Where you choose to shop can have an enormous impact on your shopping bill. It is a sad fact that with the increased interest in and demand for healthier food, some shops and supermarkets have added a tidy premium to the price of some fresh produce.

It can become easy to rack up a large shopping bill on fresh good food. However, this isn't reflective of the true cost of these goods at all. Know what is in your area and you may find an enormous price variation. Do you have a variety of different supermarkets? Do you have a local greengrocer? A local vegetable delivery scheme? Or, my top choice, a local market? I always recommend visiting a local market, as often the produce is priced honestly. There are no vast overheads to cover. No board of directors to appease. You can often walk away with bags full of fresh fruit and veg having hardly spent a thing. This produce has usually gone from grower to market stall in one to two days. That's it. This means it's packed with the micronutrients so commonly missing in today's modern diet, plus you have saved a bundle. Just look at all the options in your local area and you may be amazed at how far your money goes, and the quality that you can find.

UPCYCLE

'Upcycling' is a term that is usually applied to furniture or clothing, but I use it in relation to food too. It's all about getting creative with your leftovers. Using leftovers as part of the next meal is a great way to help your food go further. Leftover roasted veg from a Sunday roast? Throw them in a salad with some cheese and mixed leaves. Got some leftover soup? Use it as a base for a curry or as a pasta sauce. Upcycling is a simple hack, but can help you get more creative in the kitchen, and can save you money.

WHAT YOU CAN SAVE

Small savings here and there add up! By following the *Eat, Shop, Save* tips over 8 weeks you can achieve really impressive results. Here are some genuinely achievable goals based on real-life case studies from the programme.

1. HALVE YOUR WEEKLY SHOPPING BILL

2. LOSE A STONE IN WEIGHT

3. PAY FOR A FAMILY HOLIDAY

4. SAVE FOR YOUR WEDDING

5. PAY OFF A BILL

6. HELP WITH NURSERY/CHILDCARE FEES

7. FUND HOME IMPROVEMENTS

8. DE-CLUTTER AND HAVE A CAR BOOT SALE

9. JOIN A REGULAR EXERCISE GROUP

10. EAT TOGETHER AS A FAMILY

PLANNING AHEAD

To stay in the game when it comes to healthy eating, planning is the real key. Make a plan and stick to it. This checklist will steer you in the right direction.

TAKE THE TIME TO PLAN

But not too far ahead. Plan for five days – Monday to Friday – and allow yourself a little more freedom at the weekend. That DOESN'T mean go mental at the weekend, it just means you can relax a bit and maybe use the time to do some batch cooking, or cook together as a family.

SHOP THE PLAN

I know this sounds kind of obvious, but one of the biggest scourges for people wanting to stay on track with their eating, is the supermarket deal or the impulse buys. These can be the downfall of many a good intention. When you have made your meal plan, create a shopping list for those ingredients. The only extras on the list should be household items. Then, shop the list. No extras. No weird impulse buys.

DON'T LEAVE IT TO THE LAST MINUTE

Plan well in advance, such as midweek for the following week. Then you have plenty of time to get your shopping list together and get yourself sorted. It's when you leave it to the last minute that forward planning and organization start to fall apart. When you leave it too late, the temptation to say 'to hell with it' and grab something convenient like a takeaway, becomes very strong.

MEAL PLANNERS

Meal planners are easy enough to create yourself –
simply follow the template below. I recommend a
cheap chalkboard from the pound shop, but you can
use a pinboard, whiteboard or simply a piece of paper.

    To give you a helping hand, I've created eight meal
planners using the recipes from the book. You can
find these at the back of the book along with weekly
shopping lists to help you stick to budget. They focus
on evening meals only as these tend to be the main
cost for most families.

MONDAY

TUESDAY

WEDNESDAY

THURSDAY

FRIDAY

SHOPPING LIST

FRESH

....
....
....
....
....
....
....
....
....
....
....
....
....
....
....
....
....

CUPBOARD

....
....
....
....
....
....
....
....
....
....
....

SERVING SUGGESTIONS

....
....
....
....
....

BREAKFASTS

CHAPTER 1

TIPS FOR STARTING THE DAY RIGHT

I'm a real advocate of routine. Not because I'm a bore or an obsessive! It is because routines give you the best template for change. When you get into a routine it is more likely that you will develop new habits. When something is a habit, it's a behaviour that comes naturally and soon becomes the norm. Here are some of the things that I think you should try and get into your morning routine. Now, this ISN'T a full checklist. I'm also not saying do all of these things. I'm saying that the morning is an ideal time to get some healthy habits in.

REHYDRATE

While we sleep we lose a great deal of water. Just breathing gets rid of a fair old chunk of it. So when we wake up we are very likely dehydrated. Just a tiny drop in hydration can make us feel fatigued, foggy minded and groggy. On waking, down a big glass of water before you reach for the coffee.

GET ACTIVE

OK... I may be pushing it a bit here, but trust me, getting active in the morning sets your whole day up. I always do my workouts first thing. Now, this doesn't mean that you have to do a full-on gym session. It doesn't matter if you take the dog for a walk or run up and down the stairs twenty times (who cares if the kids think you are barking mad). Just do something. Your body will thank you for it and it puts you in such a great headspace for the rest of the day.

REPLACE AND SAVE

Average cost of a shop-bought latte: £2.45
Weekly cost x 5 = £12.25
Average cost of making a latte at home: 40p
Weekly cost x 5 = £2.00

Total Saving: £10.25 per week per person
Total Saving: £533 per year per person

MAKE BREAKFAST A MUST...

There is that somewhat clichéd saying that breakfast is the most important meal of the day. But there is now a lot of evidence that supports this; skipping breakfast is associated with making poorer food choices. Ploughing through your morning run on caffeine alone is also a fast track to poorer stress management, inability to focus properly and energy dips. Take the time to get breakfast down you, even if it is one you can eat on the go. We have plenty of recipes here for you.

...AND GIVE IT MORE THOUGHT

Breakfast really is the most important meal of the day, but when there is very little time in the morning, it's all too easy to skip it or grab something unhealthy. So, in addition to the breakfast recipes in this chapter, here are some extra *Eat, Shop, Save* tips to giving breakfast a little more thought... the healthy, cost-saving way. I know that, realistically, weekday breakfasts may revolve around porridge, smoothies and healthy cereals. And that's fine! Here are some super quick breakfast ideas to get something in you before you have to rush out the door. Just try not to get something from a fast-food chain as it can be expensive and can often contain some hidden nasties.

PORRIDGE

40G PORRIDGE OATS

150ML SKIMMED MILK

Make the porridge as per the packet instructions, using skimmed milk. Top with fruit or a drizzle of honey*.

*a drizzle of honey is about a teaspoon – try not to go over this, as there are a lot of calories in honey!

YOGURT AND FRUIT

250G PLAIN GREEK YOGURT

2 TABLESPOONS MIXED BERRIES OR 1 BANANA

A great breakfast on the go!

WEETABIX

2 WEETABIX

150ML SKIMMED OR SEMI-SKIMMED MILK

Weetabix is one of the healthier cereals on the market and it's always a winner with children too. If you'd prefer a different cereal, make sure it is low in sugar and high in fibre, a healthier option that will keep you fuller for longer.

TOAST AND A TOPPING

1 SLICE OF WHOLEMEAL BREAD (OR RYVITA)

YOUR FAVOURITE TOPPING: 2 TABLESPOONS PEANUT BUTTER AND HALF A BANANA; 2 TABLESPOONS BAKED BEANS; 2 TABLESPOONS PHILADELPHIA OR OTHER SPREADABLE CHEESE

Tip: Keep butter to a minimum! Did you know that half a tablespoon of butter contains 50 calories?

MINI FRITTATAS

These are a wonderful option for busy days and breakfast on the go, especially for the savoury breakfast lovers. I don't have a sweet tooth so these are right up my street. You can really put any combination of ingredients in here. They keep for 4–5 days in the fridge.

MAKES **12**

PREP **10** MINS

COOK **25** MINS

1 RED ONION, FINELY CHOPPED

OLIVE OIL

3 HANDFULS OF BABY SPINACH

8 EGGS

BUTTER, FOR GREASING

12 CHERRY TOMATOES, HALVED

200G FETA CHEESE

SALT AND PEPPER, TO TASTE

Preheat the oven to 190°C, 170°C Fan, Gas Mark 5.

Sauté the onion in a pan with a little olive oil, along with a good pinch of salt, until it has softened. Add the spinach and cook long enough for it to wilt.

Crack the eggs into a bowl with some pepper and whisk.

Grease a 12 hole muffin tray with a little butter.

Divide the onion and spinach mixture evenly between the muffin holes. Place 2 tomato halves in each hole and then top them up with the whisked egg. Crumble over the feta, again dividing it equally.

Bake for 20–25 minutes. To check if they are done, push a knife into one of the frittatas. It should come out without any liquid egg on it.

REPLACE AND SAVE
Average cost of fast food outlet breakfast x 4: £14.40
Average cost of mini frittata x 4: £4.90

Total Family Saving: £9.50

KEDGEREE

I know that kedgeree is not everyone's favourite dish, but this version will pack a nutritional punch. By simply swapping white rice for brown rice, we have ramped up the fibre content and increased the levels of B vitamins in the dish. Simple, tasty, cheap, filling and incredibly nutritious.

SERVES 4

PREP 5 MINS

COOK 30 MINS

2 KIPPER FILLETS

1 LARGE RED ONION, FINELY CHOPPED

OLIVE OIL

200G BROWN RICE

2 TEASPOONS CURRY POWDER

4 EGGS

LARGE HANDFUL OF BABY SPINACH

SALT, TO TASTE

Cook the kippers according to the packet instructions (most are boil in the bag).

Meanwhile, sauté the onion in a pan in a little olive oil, along with a good pinch of salt, until it has softened.

Add the rice and curry powder to the onion, along with enough boiling water to cover, and simmer until the rice is cooked. You may have to top the water up as you go so it doesn't boil dry, but do this little and often because the end dish shouldn't be too wet.

While the rice is cooking, hard boil the eggs (8–10 minutes). Let them cool. Remove the shells and then cut lengthways into quarters.

Once the rice is cooked, stir in the spinach and cook for long enough for it to wilt. Take off of the heat and then flake in the cooked kippers and mix everything together evenly.

Plate up and then divide the quartered boiled eggs between the plates.

CHEDDAR, TOMATO AND AVOCADO OMELETTE

Simple, yes. Tasty, absolutely! I often encourage people to start their day with a high-protein breakfast. It keeps you fuller for longer, keeps blood sugar nice and even, and of course is packed full of those all-important amino acids for growth and repair.

SERVES 1 | PREP 5 MINS | COOK 10 MINS

2 LARGE EGGS

OLIVE OIL

2 TOMATOES, DESEEDED AND ROUGHLY CHOPPED

½ RIPE AVOCADO, PITTED AND DICED

4 TABLESPOONS GRATED CHEDDAR CHEESE

PEPPER

HANDFUL OF ROCKET, TO SERVE

Crack the eggs into a bowl with some pepper and whisk.

Place a small amount of oil in a frying pan. Sauté the tomatoes for 1–2 minutes until the liquid has reduced. This intensifies their flavour. Remove them from the pan and set aside.

Add another small amount of oil to the pan and swirl it around to make sure the bottom is evenly coated. Pour in the whisked egg and cook until the egg is firm and the omelette can be moved around in the pan.

Place the cooked tomato and diced avocado on top. Sprinkle over the Cheddar and then fold the omelette in half. Cook for another 2–3 minutes so the Cheddar melts.

Serve with a rocket salad.

KIPPERS WITH SPINACH SCRAMBLE

Kippers are a love/hate ingredient. I get that. But if you are happy to eat them, they are a super cheap, quick and tasty way to get those all-important omega-3 fatty acids into your body. You could use smoked salmon here if you want, or even a cooked fish fillet of your choice, but kippers work best.

SERVES 1

PREP 5 MINS

COOK 10 MINS

1 KIPPER FILLET

2 HANDFULS OF BABY SPINACH

OLIVE OIL

2 LARGE EGGS

SALT AND PEPPER, TO TASTE

FOR THE SAUCE:

2 TEASPOONS HORSERADISH SAUCE

2 TEASPOONS MAYONNAISE

2 TEASPOONS OLIVE OIL

BLACK PEPPER, TO TASTE

Cook the kipper according to the packet instructions (most are boil in the bag).

Mix all the sauce ingredients together, stirring well, and set aside.

In a pan, sauté the spinach in a little olive oil for around a minute, or long enough for it to wilt. Crack the eggs into the pan with the spinach and keep stirring to create a scramble. Season to taste.

Place the scramble in the centre of a plate, and place the cooked kipper on top. Stir up the sauce again and drizzle over the fish.

TIP If you're only cooking for one, put spare fish fillets in the freezer for another day. You can buy spinach in handy frozen balls which are great for saving time and still nutritious.

HOMEMADE MUESLI

Homemade muesli is so easy it is ridiculous. Shop-bought mueslis can work out 6–7 times more expensive than this one gram for gram, and often have added sugar, salt and all sorts. Having a boxful of this made up in the cupboard not only saves you money but is also a healthier option.

Simply combine all the ingredients together, mix well and store in an airtight container.

500G PORRIDGE OATS

100G DATES, PITTED AND CHOPPED

300G MIXED SEEDS

100G CHOPPED MIXED NUTS

100G DRIED BERRIES (BLUEBERRIES, GOJI BERRIES, ETC.)

2 TEASPOONS CINNAMON

BERRY MUESLI LAYERS

A speedy breakfast perfect for days when you want something light and refreshing and also don't want too much mucking about. Simple, colourful, nutrient dense and tasty. Winner!

In a glass tumbler, place 1 tablespoon of muesli, followed by 1 tablespoon of yogurt, 1 teaspoon of honey, then 1 tablespoon of berries.

Repeat the layers as above until all the ingredients are used up.

3 TABLESPOONS HOMEMADE MUESLI (*SEE* ABOVE)

3 TABLESPOONS PLAIN GREEK YOGURT OR COCONUT YOGURT

2 TEASPOONS HONEY (OPTIONAL)

2 TABLESPOONS MIXED BERRIES (BLUEBERRIES, CHERRIES AND STRAWBERRIES ALL WORK GREAT)

SEEDY BREAKFAST BARS

Don't be put off by ingredients like goji berries and coconut oil. They used to be really expensive, but the ones you find in your supermarket are much more sensibly priced these days. These simple bars are perfect for breakfast on the move. Grab one out of the fridge and you're ready to go. They have all the right elements for a sustaining snack: protein, fibre, heaps of vitamins and minerals and some healthy fats. Oh… and they taste rather good too!

MAKES 12 BARS · PREP 10 MINS · CHILL 3 HOURS

8 TABLESPOONS MIXED SEEDS (FLAX, PUMPKIN, SESAME, SUNFLOWER, ETC.), PLUS EXTRA FOR SPRINKLING

3 HANDFULS OF GOJI BERRIES

HANDFUL OF PITTED DATES

4 TABLESPOONS COCOA POWDER

1 TEASPOON DESICCATED COCONUT

1 TEASPOON CINNAMON POWDER

3 TABLESPOONS COCONUT OIL OR OLIVE OIL

Place all the ingredients, except the oil, in a food processor, and pulse a few times to create a coarse paste.

Place the coconut oil in a glass bowl, if using, then sit the bowl over a pan of boiling water. The oil will melt in a matter of seconds. Add the melted oil or olive oil to the rest of the ingredients in the food processor. Blitz on high power until they've thoroughly mixed together into a smooth paste.

Add the mixture to a small cake tin or flan dish (about 25cm), and press down firmly to completely fill the tin. Sprinkle over the extra seeds.

Place in the fridge for 3 hours until set. Slice into 12 even pieces.

TIP Bulk buy mixed seeds – these store well and will save you money. You can also use raspberries, blueberries or strawberries instead of goji berries.

COCONUT AND MANGO OVERNIGHT OATS

Overnight oats have become something of a phenomenon in recent years and I suspect this is due to the fact that they are another fantastic option for busy people. If you like to be organized, this recipe is for you. Prepare this the night before and either eat before you leave in the morning or make it up in a container that you can take with you. Stress-free mornings are always a good thing. The coconut milk used here is the sort found in cartons as a regular milk replacement, rather than the stuff in cans you would use in a curry.

SERVES 1

PREP 5 MINS

CHILL 8 HOURS

40G PORRIDGE OATS

150ML COCONUT MILK

1 TABLESPOON DESICCATED COCONUT

½ RIPE MANGO, DICED

In a jar, bowl, plastic container or whatever your choice of receptacle, place the oats, coconut milk and desiccated coconut and mix well.

Place the mango on top and store in the fridge overnight.

By morning the oats will have softened ready to eat.

SMOOTHIES

200ML WATER

1 RIPE BANANA, CHOPPED

1 RIPE MANGO, DICED
(FRESH OR FROZEN)

LARGE HANDFUL OF BABY SPINACH

THE CLASSIC GREEN SMOOTHIE

Smoothies are an easy choice for breakfast as they are so simple to prepare and contain a lot of the good stuff. In recent years, smoothies have come under fire a bit due to concerns about sugar content. Some of these are valid, but ultimately it comes down to choice of ingredients. Some smoothies can contain vast amounts of apple juice for example, or low-fibre fruits which make them sugar bombs. This one on the other hand is fibre rich, low in sugar compared to off-the-shelf smoothies and is also an easy way to get your greens in. Give it a go!

Place all the ingredients in a blender and blitz into a vivid green smoothie.

NOTE You can swap the water for apple juice if you want but be aware this **WILL** notably increase the sugar content.

200ML MILK (DAIRY OR DAIRY FREE)

2 TABLESPOONS COCOA POWDER

1 TEASPOON HONEY

2 TEASPOONS INSTANT ESPRESSO,
OR ONE SHOT OF FRESH ESPRESSO

1 RIPE BANANA, CHOPPED

1 TABLESPOON PEANUT BUTTER

THE CHOCOLATE WAKE-UP

Something chocolaty for breakfast? There IS light at the end of the tunnel! Cocoa is actually an incredibly healthy ingredient, rich in magnesium and antioxidants. It also contains a substance called theobromine which is a close relative of caffeine. The addition of the coffee here gives an added kick that will get your morning off to a flying start.

Place all the ingredients in a blender and blitz into a thick smoothie with a kick.

MAKE AHEAD SNACKS AND LUNCHES

CHAPTER
2

TIPS FOR A HIGH-ENERGY DAY

One of the things I get asked about a lot is how to avoid the energy slumps that often hit us throughout the working day. So many of us get that slump after lunch, or find ourselves drifting off in the mid-morning meeting. Here are a few key tips that can help you feel more alert and keep your energy levels stable.

 ## MAKE SURE YOU HAVE BREAKFAST

As you saw in the last chapter, a good breakfast doesn't have to be a chore. You don't have to create a culinary masterpiece or measure every gram, just give yourself enough care to ensure you get a good breakfast. All the recipes we have in the breakfast chapter will keep you feeling full, will keep your blood sugar levels even and will provide you with important nutrients like B vitamins that help turn food into energy. Start the day right and you are on your way to a feel-good day.

 ## STAY HYDRATED

OK, this may seem like a recurrent theme, but for good reason. Even a slight drop in hydration can lead to an enormous drop in energy, mental performance and clarity. Despite what you may read, there isn't actually a magic number of glasses of water you should drink a day. Your body will be the best barometer and it's all to do with the colour of your pee. Try and drink enough water so that your urine runs clear, then stop. This means you are hydrated. When your urine starts to get colour back, drink a little more. This is your body telling you exactly where you are at. Stick to this and you will be in the right zone.

REPLACE AND SAVE

Average cost of buying your lunch out is £6 a day (£30 for an average 5-day working week).
Over 15 years that adds up £20,000!
Average cost of Dale's lunches: £3 a day (£15 for an average 5-day working week).

Total Saving: a whopping 50%!

3. AVOID THE CRASH-AND-BURN FOODS

While it may be tempting to reach for sweet sugary treats when your energy is flagging, it is completely counterproductive. These foods send our blood sugar levels up super high, which feels great at first. But it isn't great for our body. If blood sugar is too high or too low it can be life-threatening, so our body has very tightly controlled ways of dealing with this. When our blood sugar rises, we release the hormone insulin. Insulin tells our cells that glucose is available to turn into energy, and the cells open their doorways so that the glucose can get inside and do its job. The more blood sugar rises, and the quicker it rises, the stronger the insulin response that takes place. Now, refined sugary foods like sweets, chocolate, pastries and cakes release vast amounts of sugar into our blood very quickly. Whilst this feels like it gives us a boost, our body responds by aggressively releasing insulin to get that high blood sugar down again. This causes our blood sugar to crash and, guess what, we feel exhausted and like we are having to drag ourselves through the day.

4. BALANCE BLOOD SUGAR

One of the worst things for making our energy levels roller coaster throughout the day is poor blood sugar control. When our blood sugar rises we feel great, when it plummets we feel terrible and exhausted. Starting your day with a good breakfast consisting of low-glycaemic carbohydrates and some high-quality protein is the place to start. This combination means your meal will release its energy slowly and gradually, keeping your blood sugar, and in turn your energy levels, nice and stable. The same principles apply to lunch also. See the recipes in this chapter for great ideas, but the same rule of a complex carbohydrate with some good-quality protein and plenty of fresh vegetables is the way to go. This creates a meal that drip feeds us glucose, meaning there is a constant, gentle supply available for energy production.

5. SNACK SMARTER

So, with number 3 above in mind, what makes a better snack choice? I always say that protein-based snacks rule the roost here. These really keep blood sugar stable and stave off hunger. My top choices are nuts, seeds, mini cheeses, cooked meats and hard-boiled eggs. See page 148 for some more ideas.

BATCH SAUCE

This is such a great base sauce for anything from pasta to ratatouille. Even to top a pizza. Whip this up and freeze it in portions. If you place the portions in ziplock bags, you can stack them like envelopes in the freezer.

2 LARGE RED ONIONS, FINELY CHOPPED

5 GARLIC CLOVES, FINELY CHOPPED

2 RED PEPPERS, DESEEDED AND CHOPPED

1 COURGETTE, SLICED

OLIVE OIL

6 LARGE TOMATOES, QUARTERED

680G PASSATA

SALT, TO TASTE

In a pan, sauté the onions, garlic, peppers and courgette in a little olive oil, along with a good pinch of salt, until they have started to soften.

Throw in the fresh tomatoes and continue to cook for another 2–3 minutes.

Add the passata and simmer for another 5–6 minutes before transferring to a blender, or using a hand blender, to purée into a smooth sauce.

TIP Puréed veg is a great way to get healthy stuff on the plate. Try my other 'hidden veg' sauces, such as the one in Fallon's Chicken Curry on page 116.

DIPS

SERVES 4 · PREP 5 MINS · COOK 0 MINS

1 X 400G CAN OF BUTTER BEANS, DRAINED

1 X 400G CAN CANNELLINI BEANS, LIQUID RETAINED

1 GARLIC CLOVE, FINELY CHOPPED

½ SMALL CHILLI, FINELY CHOPPED

JUICE OF 1 LARGE LIME

½ TEASPOON GROUND CUMIN

SALT, TO TASTE

LIMEY WHITE BEAN SPREAD

White beans give the most incredible, creamy texture. This dip is wonderful in sandwiches or dolloped on top of some roasted sweet potato wedges.

Place all the ingredients in a blender or food processor and blend into a smooth spread. If you need to thin out the texture, just add a little water.

---

2 LARGE RIPE AVOCADOS, HALVED AND PITTED (MAKE SURE THEY ARE SOFT WHEN SQUEEZED)

2 GARLIC CLOVES, FINELY CHOPPED

½ LARGE RED ONION, FINELY CHOPPED

2 SMALL CHILLIES, FINELY CHOPPED

BUNCH OF FRESH CORIANDER, ROUGHLY CHOPPED

JUICE OF 1 LIME

1 TABLESPOON EXTRA VIRGIN OLIVE OIL

SALT, TO TASTE

GUACAMOLE

If you are buying that fluorescent-green ready-made guacamole from the supermarket, what are you doing? It's horrible and a fresh guacamole is so easy to make. This version packs huge amounts of flavour as well as a massive nutritional punch.

Scoop the avocado flesh into a bowl and mash with a fork. Add the garlic, onion, chillies, coriander, lime juice, olive oil and salt, and mix together well. Store in an airtight container in the fridge for up to 2 days.

---

2 X 400G CANS OF CHICKPEAS, ONE DRAINED, ONE WITH LIQUID RETAINED

2 GARLIC CLOVES, ROUGHLY CHOPPED

2 TABLESPOONS TAHINI

JUICE OF 1 LARGE LEMON

SALT, TO TASTE

HUMMUS

Shop-bought hummus often contains processed oils, and more oil than is necessary, meaning it can be a bit of a calorie bomb. Making it yourself means you can make it tastier, lighter and cheaper. It keeps for 4–5 days in an airtight container in the fridge.

Place all the ingredients in a blender or food processor and blitz until smooth. If you feel you need any more liquid, just add a little water.

BACON, AVOCADO AND ROCKET WRAP

This is so fresh and flavoursome, and the combination of bacon and avocado is a match made in heaven. The crispiness of the bacon combined with the silky avocado is just wonderful.

SERVES 1 | PREP 5 MINS | COOK 5 MINS

3 SMOKED BACON RASHERS

½ VERY RIPE AVOCADO, PITTED

JUICE OF ¼ LEMON

1 WHOLEWHEAT TORTILLA

2 HANDFULS OF ROCKET

SALT AND PEPPER, TO TASTE

Preheat the grill.

Cook the bacon under the grill (or in the oven), long enough to get crispy edges.

Meanwhile, scoop the avocado flesh into a bowl. Squeeze in the lemon juice, add a little salt and pepper, and mash.

Spread the mashed avocado down the centre of the tortilla. Place the cooked bacon on top of the avocado mash, then the rocket on top of the bacon.

Roll up the tortilla tightly and wrap in foil or clingfilm.

TIP Cut costs by making this a veggie wrap – substitute the bacon for some juicy tomatoes; a classic pairing with avocado.

SIMPLE PASTA SALAD

A pasta salad is a portable lunch staple, but when you look at the ingredients in a lot of the shop-bought ones, it is like reading the contents of a chemistry set. With such a simple dish there really is no need, and you can make a super flavoursome version without all of the nasties. If olives and anchovies aren't your thing, then swap them for another of your favourite vegetables and tuna instead.

SERVES 1 | PREP 5 MINS | COOK 10 MINS

70G WHOLEWHEAT FUSILLI PASTA

2 LARGE TOMATOES

1 TABLESPOON SLICED BLACK OLIVES FROM A JAR

4–5 ANCHOVIES

¼ RED ONION, FINELY CHOPPED

HANDFUL OF BABY SPINACH, SHREDDED

PINCH OF MIXED HERBS

50G FETA CHEESE

SALT AND PEPPER, TO TASTE

Cook the pasta until al dente, or according to the packet instructions. Drain and transfer to a lunch box.

Chop the tomatoes really finely, making sure that all the juice doesn't run away. Add the tomatoes and their juice to the cooked pasta.

Add the olives, anchovies, chopped onion, shredded spinach and mixed herbs and mix together well.

Crumble over the feta.

Add salt and pepper to taste – but remember that the anchovies and feta are already quite salty, so don't overdo it.

CHICKEN, YOGURT AND LIME WRAP

This is a cool, zesty, quick make-ahead lunch. You could throw in any accompanying vegetables with this really, but this combo seems to work the best.

SERVES 1 | PREP 10 MINS | COOK 0 MINS

SMALL HANDFUL OF BABY SPINACH

1 WHOLEWHEAT TORTILLA

1 CARROT, GRATED

½ CUCUMBER, CUT INTO THIN SPEARS

SMALL BUNCH OF FRESH CORIANDER, COARSELY TORN

½ SMALL CHILLI, SLICED (OPTIONAL)

FOR THE CHICKEN

2 TABLESPOONS PLAIN GREEK YOGURT

ZEST AND JUICE OF 1 LIME

1 PRE-COOKED CHICKEN BREAST, SLICED

SALT AND PEPPER, TO TASTE

To make the chicken filling, combine the yogurt and lime juice and zest and mix well. Add the sliced chicken and mix well again to ensure it is evenly coated. Season to taste.

Assemble the wrap by laying the spinach down the centre of the tortilla. Top with the grated carrot, the cucumber, then the chicken, the coriander, and finally the sliced chilli, if using, before rolling it up tightly and wrapping in foil or clingfilm.

TIP Save time by making extra filling for future lunches. Store in the fridge in an airtight container.

CHICKPEA, TOMATO AND CORIANDER SALAD

Back to that store cupboard staple – tinned pulses.
These make preparing a healthy meal an absolute walk
in the park. Stress free and super fast.

SERVES 1 • PREP 10 MINS • COOK 0 MINS

1 X 400G CAN OF CHICKPEAS, DRAINED

¼ RED ONION, FINELY CHOPPED

½ CUCUMBER, DICED

7–8 CHERRY TOMATOES, HALVED

SMALL BUNCH OF FRESH CORIANDER, ROUGHLY CHOPPED

FOR THE DRESSING:

JUICE OF 1 LIME

1 TABLESPOON OLIVE OIL

½ TEASPOON GARLIC POWDER

SALT AND PEPPER, TO TASTE

Place all the salad ingredients in a lunch box and mix well.

Mix all the dressing ingredients in a small container and keep aside until you are ready to eat, as the salad is at its best when freshly dressed.

TIP Tinned chickpeas are a great addition to your store cupboard for speedy lunches. Black beans, butter beans, lentils and couscous are other handy go-to essentials.

VEGETABLE FRITTATA

Frittatas are one of the best portable meals. They taste great cold and are so diverse – you can pretty much add what you like. This mixed veg version is perfect as it contains protein, healthy fats and non-starchy vegetables to keep you feeling satisfied and properly fuelled all afternoon.

SERVES 2 | PREP 5 MINS | COOK 15 MINS

½ RED ONION, FINELY CHOPPED

½ COURGETTE, SLICED

OLIVE OIL

LARGE HANDFUL OF BABY SPINACH

3 LARGE EGGS

40G GOAT'S CHEESE (OR ANY CHEESE OF YOUR CHOICE)

MIXED LEAF SALAD, TO SERVE

SALT, TO TASTE

Begin by sautéing the onion and courgette in a small ovenproof pan in a little olive oil, along with a pinch of salt, until the onion has softened. Add the baby spinach and sauté until it wilts.

Preheat the grill.

Whisk the eggs in a bowl. Pour the whisked eggs over the cooked vegetables and cook until you see the edges begin to firm up, but there is still uncooked egg in the centre of the pan.

Crumble over the cheese.

At this point, place the pan under the hot grill until the egg is cooked through.

Leave to cool before placing half the frittata in a lunch box with a mixed leaf salad. Leftovers can be stored in the fridge ready for lunch the following day.

CHICKEN AND BLUE CHEESE SALAD

This is one of my all-time favourite salads. It does have quite a high fat content but don't freak out! Fat can help to keep us feeling full and satisfied, so we eat less. But remember – moderation is key.

SERVES 1 | PREP 10 MINS | COOK 0 MINS

2 HANDFULS OF BABY SPINACH

½ CUCUMBER, SLICED

½ RED PEPPER, DESEEDED AND SLICED

4-5 CHERRY TOMATOES, HALVED

1 PRE-COOKED CHICKEN BREAST, SLICED

50G BLUE CHEESE

FOR THE DRESSING

1 TEASPOON WHITE WINE VINEGAR

1 TABLESPOON MAYONNAISE

2 TEASPOONS OLIVE OIL

½ TEASPOON GARLIC POWDER

In a lunch box combine the spinach, cucumber, pepper and tomatoes. Lay the chicken on top and crumble over the blue cheese.

Mix all the dressing ingredients in a small container and keep aside until you are ready to eat, as the salad is at its best when freshly dressed.

TIP Examples of good fats to include in your diet are: oily fish, nuts and seeds. See my handy list on page 11.

HUMMUS, BEETROOT AND FETA PITTA POCKET

This is such a satisfying and nutritious sandwich that has so many different flavour elements. The colour is pretty wild too.

SERVES 1 · PREP 10 MINS · COOK 3 MINS

2 SMALL PRE-PACKED COOKED BEETROOT (NOT THE PICKLED VARIETY)

2 TABLESPOONS SHOP-BOUGHT HUMMUS, OR *SEE* RECIPE ON PAGE 47

50G FETA CHEESE

1 WHOLEWHEAT PITTA

SMALL HANDFUL OF MIXED SALAD LEAVES

Preheat the grill.

In a bowl, roughly mash the beetroot. Add the hummus and mix the two together. Crumble in the feta, and mix again.

Place the pitta under the grill for 2–3 minutes until warm. This will help you to carefully cut along one edge to open the pitta out to make a pocket.

Line one side of the inside of the pitta with the salad leaves.

Dollop in the hummus, beetroot and feta mixture and press down to fill the pitta and pack it tightly.

MACKEREL SALAD WITH HORSERADISH HONEY DRESSING

This simple salad is gorgeous and is a great way to add more oily fish to your diet. Oily fish is one of the healthiest foods around due to the omega-3 fatty acids that it contains, which are important for the health of the heart, the eyes, the skin, and for reducing inflammation. This salad uses pre-cooked mackerel fillets that can be found in your supermarket.

¼ CUCUMBER, SLICED

½ RED PEPPER, DESEEDED AND SLICED LENGTHWAYS

HANDFUL OF BABY SPINACH

HANDFUL OF ROCKET

1 SMALL PRE-PACKED COOKED BEETROOT, DICED

1 PRE-COOKED PEPPERED MACKEREL FILLET

FOR THE DRESSING:

2 TEASPOONS HORSERADISH SAUCE

1 TEASPOON LEMON JUICE OR BALSAMIC VINEGAR

1 TEASPOON HONEY

1 TEASPOON OLIVE OIL

Place all the salad vegetables in a lunch box, then flake the mackerel fillet into the salad.

For the best taste and texture, make the dressing in a separate pot or jar to dress the salad just before serving. Simply add all the dressing ingredients together and mix well.

MIXED BEAN CHILLI

I do enjoy a good chilli. I love the meat variety and I love vegetarian versions too, and this mixed bean one won't disappoint.

1 RED ONION, FINELY CHOPPED

1 RED CHILLI, FINELY CHOPPED

OLIVE OIL

2½ RED PEPPERS, FINELY CHOPPED

2 X 400G CANS OF MIXED BEANS, DRAINED

2 X 400G CANS OF CHOPPED TOMATOES

2 TABLESPOONS GROUND CUMIN

2 HEAPED TEASPOONS SMOKED PAPRIKA

SALT AND PEPPER, TO TASTE

BROWN RICE, TO SERVE

In a pan, sauté the onion and chilli in a little olive oil, along with a good pinch of salt, until the onions have softened.

Add the peppers, beans and tomatoes and simmer for 15 minutes. Add the spices and simmer for a further 15 minutes, stirring often, to create a thick, rich sauce.

Taste and add more salt or spices if needed. Serve with brown rice.

CHICKEN KEBAB

When you have had a long day, the temptation to divert via the kebab house on your way home from work may be high. Once in a while is no problem at all, but getting into the regular habit of this can soon take its toll on your waistline and your wallet. This fresh, tasty version will scratch that itch, takes no effort at all and is a fraction of the cost.

SERVES 1 · PREP 5 MINS · COOK 25 MINS

1 CHICKEN BREAST

2 TABLESPOONS GREEK YOGURT

50G FETA CHEESE

1 LARGE WHOLEMEAL PITTA

1 LARGE TOMATO, SLICED

¼ RED ONION, SLICED LENGTHWAYS

1 OREGANO SPRIG

SALT AND PEPPER, TO TASTE

Preheat the oven to 180°C, 160°C Fan, Gas Mark 4.

Place the chicken breast on a baking tray and season with a little salt and pepper. Cook in the oven for 20–25 minutes.

Whilst the chicken is cooking, place the yogurt in a bowl. Crumble in the feta cheese and season with a little pepper. Mash together with a fork.

Place the pitta in the oven for around a minute, just long enough to warm it. Cut along one side to make a pocket.

Remove the chicken from the oven and cut into slices.

Line one side of the inside of the pitta with the tomato slices, add the sliced chicken and then the sliced onion. Top with the yogurt and feta mixture and sprinkle over the oregano leaves.

REPLACE AND SAVE
Average cost of a takeaway kebab x 4 = £20
Average cost of Dale's kebab x 4 = £10

Total Family Saving: £10

CLASSIC GREEK SALAD

This is the crowd-pleaser of salads that conjures up memories of Mediterranean getaways … or maybe it just tastes really good.

SERVES 1 · PREP 10 MINS · COOK 0 MINS

2 HANDFULS OF MIXED SALAD LEAVES

½ CUCUMBER, DICED

4-5 PLUM TOMATOES, ROUGHLY CHOPPED

¼ RED ONION, SLICED

2 TABLESPOONS BLACK OLIVES, PITTED

100G FETA CHEESE, CUBED

FOR THE DRESSING

1 TABLESPOON OLIVE OIL

2 TEASPOONS LEMON JUICE

½ TEASPOON DRIED OREGANO

SALT AND PEPPER, TO TASTE

This is a simple one – mix all the salad ingredients together in a lunch box. Whisk the dressing ingredients together and dress the salad just before serving. The best things are always the simplest!

SIMPLE AFTER WORK SUPPERS

CHAPTER
3

TIPS FOR SMART SHOPPING

 ### 1. GET LOOSE

Every time we buy something that's washed, cut and ready-prepared, we're paying for that convenience. Always check whether it's cheaper to buy loose ingredients than packaged. Try to buy fruit and vegetables at a local market. Pre-grated cheese, pre-chopped veg and any 'ready to eat' ingredients all come with a higher price tag.

 ### 2. LOOK AROUND YOU

Face-level shelves are the most appealing to a consumer and therefore supermarkets put the more expensive produce on them. Choose from the lower or higher shelves. Remember: easy-grab height – think twice. Always look at the supermarket label for the price per unit (e.g. £1 per 100g).

 ### 3. TRACK YOUR SPENDING

Write it all down – everything. You'll be able to see what you're spending and where you can save. Make sure you take into account top-ups: extra shops, eating out, paying for lunch out, etc. Now, taking this into account, give yourself a realistic weekly shopping budget and stick to it.

 ### 4. DON'T FALL FOR SUPERMARKET THEATRE

When it comes to supermarket food, always read the fine print. Some ingredients appear 'fresh' but a display food counter can be a piece of 'supermarket theatre'. Check to see whether goods have been frozen before. Do your maths and make sure the special offers are worthwhile – buy-one-get-one-free offers and multi-buys are not always as appealing as they originally seem.

 ### 5. TRY THE TASTE TEST

We love our favourite brands, but can you really tell the difference between heavily marketed products and own-brand equivalents? Not only do some popular brands have increased sugar and salt content, but they can also stretch the purse strings. Buy own-label brands and you can cut your weekly shopping bill by 50 per cent.

EMBRACE THE FREEZER!

You can find some great bargains in the freezer section of your supermarket. Frozen fish is a perfect example – it is actually just as fresh (if not fresher) than the fish in the fridge section, which has usually been previously frozen anyway! Also consider frozen fruit and veg and even meat. The products available now are better than ever, and just as nutritious as their fresh, more expensive, equivalents.

PLAN, PLAN, PLAN

One of the main ways that you and your family can save money is by being savvy with your weekly food shop. Follow these steps and you won't go far wrong!

STEP ONE
Use your weekly meal-planner board.
Plan a meal for each evening of the week and write it on your board (see page 19 for more info).

STEP TWO
Make a list.
Look up the ingredients lists for all the recipes, and make a list of everything you'll need.

We've made these first two steps super easy by providing you with eight weeks' worth of meal planners and shopping lists. See pages 188–203!

STEP THREE
Think about breakfasts, lunches and snacks.
Plan ahead a week's worth of breakfasts, lunches and even snacks and add to your shopping list exactly what you will need. Your aim is to avoid any excuse to buy your meals while you're out and about, because this will really add up and make it harder to save money. Instead, buy the ingredients to make everything you need at home.

STEP FOUR
Hit the shops!
Stick to your shopping list so you only buy exactly what you need. Don't get tempted by offers, or anything else that is not on your list.

And remember...
...to factor into your meal planners when you will be using leftovers from your batch cooking, so you make your weekly shop even cheaper!

REPLACE AND SAVE

Follow the tips above and see if you can halve your weekly shopping bill.

QUESADILLAS

I absolutely adore quesadillas. They tick all the right boxes – delicious, comforting, easy and good for you. Winner! This dish calls for refried beans, which can easily be found in any supermarket.

SERVES 1 · **PREP 5 MINS** · **COOK 10 MINS**

2 SOFT TORTILLAS

2 TABLESPOONS REFRIED BEANS

5–6 JALAPEÑO SLICES (OPTIONAL)

SMALL HANDFUL OF BABY SPINACH

2 TABLESPOONS GRATED CHEDDAR CHEESE

Preheat the oven to 180°C, 160°C Fan, Gas Mark 4.

Place one tortilla on a baking tray. Spread the refried beans over the tortilla. If using the jalapeños, scatter them over now, then add the spinach.

Top with the grated Cheddar and place the second tortilla on top to create a sandwich, then press down firmly to pack in and flatten the filling.

Place in the oven for 8–10 minutes, until the tortilla is toasted and golden and the cheese has melted.

REPLACE AND SAVE
Average cost of chain restaurant quesadillas x 4 = £18
Average cost of Dale's quesadillas x 4 = £4

Total Family Saving: £7

STEAK WITH PEA AND FETA MASH AND SWEET POTATO WEDGES

This simple, speedy dinner is satisfying on so many levels.

SERVES 1 · PREP 5 MINS · COOK 25 MINS

½ SWEET POTATO, CUT INTO WEDGES

OLIVE OIL

5 TABLESPOONS FROZEN PEAS

80G FETA CHEESE

1 SIRLOIN STEAK

PEPPER, TO TASTE

Place the sweet potato wedges on a baking tray, drizzle over a little olive oil and roast for 20–25 minutes until soft with golden brown edges.

Meanwhile, place the peas in a saucepan, cover with boiling water and simmer until soft enough to crush.

Drain the peas and mash them with a fork. Crumble in the feta cheese along with some pepper.

Pan fry the steak to taste.

TIP To make this delicious dinner even more economical, you could shop around for budget beef cuts such as skirt and top rump – if in doubt, ask your butcher!

NORTH AFRICAN SPICED VEGETABLES, COUSCOUS AND HALLOUMI

OK, so a mixture of Mediterranean elements here. But this dish is really simple, an absolute flavour bomb, and very nutrient dense and satisfying. A sure-fire favourite in the making.

SERVES 4 | PREP 5 MINS | COOK 35 MINS

1 LARGE RED ONION, HALVED AND SLICED LENGTHWAYS

4 GARLIC CLOVES, FINELY CHOPPED

OLIVE OIL

1 RED PEPPER, DESEEDED AND DICED

1 YELLOW PEPPER, DESEEDED AND DICED

1 LARGE COURGETTE, CUT INTO HALF CIRCLES

1 SMALL AUBERGINE, DICED

400G TOMATO PASSATA

2 TEASPOONS CUMIN

1 TEASPOON SMOKED PAPRIKA

250G COUSCOUS

1 TEASPOON STOCK POWDER

250G HALLOUMI CHEESE

SALT AND PEPPER, TO TASTE

In a large saucepan, sauté the onion and garlic in a little olive oil, along with a good pinch of salt, until the onion begins to soften.

Add the remaining vegetables, mix well, and continue to cook for 7–8 minutes until the veg begins to soften.

Add the passata and simmer for around 15–20 minutes, until the liquid has reduced and the veg is completely cooked. At this stage, add the spices and taste. If you feel it needs more spice or seasoning, now is the time to do it.

While the veg is simmering, place the couscous in a bowl with the stock powder and add enough boiling water to cover it by about 1cm. Cover the bowl with a tea towel and let it sit until ready to serve.

Slice the halloumi width ways into 8 equal slices. Gently pan fry until golden on each side.

Plate up with the couscous in the centre, dollop on a generous helping of the vegetables, then place the halloumi on top. Divine!

SALMON FOIL PARCELS WITH SWEET POTATO WEDGES

This is one of the most faff-free recipes imaginable, with both the salmon and the sweet potato wedges cooking for about the same amount of time. Despite its simplicity, it is incredibly flavoursome, with plenty of complex carbs, protein, omega-3 fatty acids and fibre.

SERVES 1

PREP 5 MINS

COOK 20 MINS

1 SWEET POTATO, SKIN ON, CUT INTO WEDGES

OLIVE OIL

1 SALMON FILLET

1 GARLIC CLOVE, ROUGHLY CHOPPED

1 GREEN CHILLI, CHOPPED

1-CM PIECE OF FRESH ROOT GINGER, SLICED

JUICE OF ½ LIME

2 TEASPOONS SOY SAUCE

SMALL HANDFUL OF FRESH CORIANDER, COARSELY TORN

Preheat the oven to 180°C, 160°C Fan, Gas Mark 4.

Place the sweet potato wedges on a baking tray and drizzle with a small amount of olive oil. Bake in the oven for 20 minutes, until soft and turning golden at the edges. The salmon will soon be in the oven at the same time, so 20 minutes is the total cooking time.

Whilst the wedges are in the oven, make the parcels. Using tin foil or greaseproof paper, create a boat shape. It needs to be big enough to hold the salmon fillet and also leak-proof so the liquids don't escape. Place the parcel on a baking tray.

Place the salmon fillet in the parcel, along with the garlic, chilli, ginger, lime juice and soy sauce. Seal the parcel by scrunching the edges of the foil or paper together.

Move the sweet potato wedges down a shelf if necessary, and place the salmon parcel in the oven for around 12–15 minutes. Both the salmon and the sweet potato wedges should be done at the same time. The salmon should be lightly cooked and sitting in a well-flavoured broth.

Scatter over the coriander just before serving.

NUTTY LEMON GRASS CHICKEN

This delicious dish, packed with glorious Southeast Asian flavours, is a true crowd-pleaser.

SERVES 4

PREP 5 MINS

COOK 35 MINS

BATCH

1 RED ONION, SLICED

5 GARLIC CLOVES, FINELY CHOPPED

2 STICKS OF LEMON GRASS, BASHED

1 GREEN CHILLI, FINELY CHOPPED

OLIVE OIL

2 X 400ML CANS OF COCONUT MILK

2 HEAPED TABLESPOONS PEANUT BUTTER

1 TEASPOON GROUND TURMERIC

4 CHICKEN BREASTS, DICED

2 LARGE HANDFULS OF BABY SPINACH

JUICE OF 1 LIME

SALT, TO TASTE

In a pan, sauté the onion, garlic, lemon grass and chilli in a little olive oil, along with a good pinch of salt, until the onion has softened.

Add the coconut milk and stir in the peanut butter and turmeric and simmer for around 10 minutes until the sauce starts to thicken and the flavour of the lemon grass really begins to penetrate the dish.

Add the diced chicken and continue to simmer for around 15 minutes until cooked through.

Add the spinach and allow it to wilt before squeezing in the lime juice.

PASTA ARRABBIATA

This gorgeous dish is pasta with a little kick. If there are people in the family who are sensitive souls when it comes to spice, then you can reduce the chilli or even leave it out. If not, go all in and see how lovely this dish is. Remember – always use wholewheat pasta for its higher fibre content.

SERVES 4

PREP 5 MINS

COOK 25 MINS

300G WHOLEWHEAT PASTA
(PENNE OR FUSILLI)

1 LARGE RED ONION,
FINELY CHOPPED

3 GARLIC CLOVES, FINELY CHOPPED

1 GREEN CHILLI, FINELY CHOPPED

OLIVE OIL

2 X 400G CANS OF CHOPPED
TOMATOES

40G SLICED BLACK OLIVES
FROM A JAR

1 TABLESPOON RED WINE

SALT, TO TASTE

Place the pasta in a saucepan and cover with boiling water. Cook until al dente or according to the packet instructions. Drain and set aside.

In a second saucepan, sauté the onion, garlic and chilli in a little olive oil, along with a good pinch of of salt, until the onion has softened.

Add the tomatoes, olives and red wine and simmer for around 20 minutes. You want the sauce to thicken and reduce in volume. This gives a much greater intensity of flavour and the extra time is so worth it.

Add the cooked pasta to the sauce and mix well before serving.

SPANISH CHICKEN

This simple dish is one that I predict will become a favourite in many households. It is absolutely gorgeous, and the flavours... wow! It's also a chance to get your hands a bit mucky and have some fun in the kitchen. Everything cooks together in one roasting tin too so minimal fuss.

SERVES 4 | PREP 10 MINS | COOK 45 MINS

4 CHICKEN LEGS

2 LARGE SWEET POTATOES, SKIN ON, CUT INTO WEDGES

2 LARGE RED ONIONS, HALVED AND SLICED LENGTHWAYS

2 RED PEPPERS, DESEEDED AND SLICED LENGTHWAYS

2 TABLESPOONS OLIVE OIL

2 ROSEMARY SPRIGS

2½ TEASPOONS SMOKED PAPRIKA

SALT AND PEPPER, TO TASTE

SALAD, TO SERVE

Preheat the oven to 180°C, 160°C Fan, Gas Mark 4.

Place the chicken, sweet potatoes, onions and peppers in a large rectangular roasting tin.

Drizzle over the olive oil and throw in the rosemary. Season with salt and pepper then roll up your sleeves and get your hands in. Toss together to make sure everything is evenly coated.

Place the tray in the oven and bake for 25 minutes. Remove and sprinkle over the paprika before placing back in the oven for a further 20 minutes. Stir occasionally to avoid sticking. What you want to end up with is the sweet potatoes nice and soft, the onions and peppers all caramelized together and a gorgeous sauce.

Serve with a salad.

KALE AND MUSHROOM STIR-FRIED RICE

This is a great all-in-one dish that will fill you up with the good stuff and is light and easy to cook. This calls for a packet of pre-cooked brown rice, a great ingredient to keep in your store cupboard.

SERVES 4

PREP 5 MINS

COOK 20 MINS

1 RED ONION, HALVED THEN SLICED

4 GARLIC CLOVES, FINELY CHOPPED

OLIVE OIL

180G CURLY KALE

100G CHESTNUT MUSHROOMS, SLICED

1 X 250G PACKET OF PRE-COOKED BROWN RICE

4 TEASPOONS SOY SAUCE

1 TABLESPOON HONEY

4 TEASPOONS CURRY POWDER

2 TEASPOONS SESAME OIL

1 TABLESPOON PEANUT BUTTER

SALT, TO TASTE

In a pan, sauté the onion and garlic in a little olive oil, along with a good pinch of salt, until the onion has softened.

Add the kale and mushrooms and stir-fry until the kale wilts and the mushrooms soften.

Add the rice, soy sauce, honey, curry powder, sesame oil and peanut butter and mix well until the rice is heated through.

TIP Vegetables are often at their cheapest when they're in season. Why not try substituting kale for cabbage or spinach during winter?

FRUITY FISH FAJITAS

People often associate fajitas with chicken, but fish is a great option and it's something we should be eating more of. Cod can be quite expensive now, but another white fish has popped up that is cheaper and more sustainable – basa. You can find it in most supermarkets.

SERVES 4

PREP 5 MINS

COOK 20 MINS

4 WHITE FISH FILLETS, SUCH AS COD OR BASA, HALVED

2 TEASPOONS MEXICAN SEASONING

8 FLOUR TORTILLAS

2 HANDFULS OF BABY SPINACH

1 RIPE MANGO, DICED

1 RED ONION, FINELY CHOPPED

1 X 125G BALL OF MOZZARELLA CHEESE

Preheat the oven to 180°C, 160°C Fan, Gas Mark 4.

Place the fish in a bowl. Sprinkle over the Mexican Seasoning and mix well to ensure the fish is fully coated. Spread the fish out evenly on a baking tray, and bake in the oven for around 20 minutes.

To assemble the fajitas, take a tortilla and add some baby spinach, followed by some of the cooked fish, diced mango and onion. Roughly tear the mozzarella and place some on top of the other fillings. Roll up the tortilla tightly.

CHICKEN AND HALLOUMI KEBABS WITH WHITE BEAN SALAD

This dish calls for one of those store cupboard staples that can be a real lifesaver – tinned beans. They are such a great thing to stock up on as in a matter of minutes you can throw together a delicious meal with minimal effort. Wooden kebab skewers can be found in your supermarket.

SERVES 4

PREP 10 MINS

COOK 20 MINS

4 CHICKEN BREASTS, CUBED

2 RED PEPPERS, DESEEDED AND CUT INTO 2-CM SQUARES

225G HALLOUMI CHEESE, CUT INTO 12 CUBES

2 X 400G CANS OF CANNELLINI BEANS, DRAINED

8–10 CHERRY TOMATOES, HALVED

½ RED ONION, FINELY CHOPPED

2 HANDFULS OF MIXED SALAD LEAVES

2 TEASPOONS DRIED MIXED HERBS

SALT AND PEPPER, TO TASTE

1 LEMON, CUT INTO QUARTER WEDGES, TO SERVE

Preheat the oven to 190°C, 170°C Fan, Gas Mark 5.

Using 8–12 wooden kebab skewers, make the kebabs by threading a cube of chicken breast, then a slice of pepper, then a cube of halloumi, and repeat this sequence a second time. Do this with the remaining skewers, until all the ingredients are used up.

Place the kebabs on a foil-lined baking tray and season with a little salt and pepper – but remember that the halloumi is already quite salty so don't overdo it. Place in the oven and bake for 20 minutes, turning once halfway through.

Whilst the kebabs are cooking, mix together the drained beans, cherry tomatoes, onion, salad leaves and mixed herbs, and add a little salt and pepper to taste.

To serve, place a mound of the bean salad in the centre of each plate and place 2–3 kebabs across it. Squeeze over the lemon before serving.

PRAWN AND CHORIZO MASH-UP

This is a lovely flavoursome one-pan dish that is great for using up leftovers.

SERVES 4

PREP 10 MINS

COOK 20 MINS

1 LARGE RED ONION, HALVED THEN SLICED LENGTHWAYS

4 GARLIC CLOVES, FINELY CHOPPED

130G CHORIZO SAUSAGE, DICED

1 LARGE COURGETTE, CUT INTO HALF CIRCLES

1 RED PEPPER, DESEEDED AND CHOPPED

1 ORANGE PEPPER, DESEEDED AND CHOPPED

1 TEASPOON SMOKED PAPRIKA

300G COOKED PEELED KING PRAWNS

Sauté the onion, garlic and chorizo in a saucepan. You won't need additional oil in this dish as the heat will quickly draw out the oil in the chorizo. Once the onion begins to soften, add the remaining vegetables and the smoked paprika and cook for a further 10 minutes until the vegetables have softened.

Add the prawns and cook for another 2–3 minutes before serving.

TIP Remember to check frozen ingredients in your supermarket. Frozen prawns can be bought in bulk and are great to keep to hand in the freezer.

GOOEY BAKED RATATOUILLE

**This is pure comfort food and tastes like heaven.
Also, you'd struggle to find an easier dish.**

SERVES 4 · PREP 10 MINS · COOK 35 MINS

2 LARGE RED ONIONS, FINELY CHOPPED

4 GARLIC CLOVES, FINELY CHOPPED

OLIVE OIL

2 LARGE COURGETTES, DICED

1 LARGE RED PEPPER, DESEEDED AND DICED

1 SMALL AUBERGINE, DICED

600G TOMATO PASSATA

200G MATURE CHEDDAR CHEESE, GRATED

SALT, TO TASTE

SALAD, TO SERVE

Preheat the oven to 180°C, 160°C Fan, Gas Mark 4.

Sauté the onions and garlic in a little olive oil, along with a good pinch of salt, until the onions begin to soften. Throw in the rest of the vegetables and continue to cook for 5 minutes until the vegetables begin to soften.

Add the passata and simmer for 20 minutes or so, stirring constantly. You want the ratatouille to thicken and all the liquid to reduce down to create a thick luscious texture.

Transfer the ratatouille to a large oven dish, or 4 small heat-proof dishes, and top with the grated Cheddar. Bake in the oven until the cheese melts and starts to bubble.

Serve with a salad.

HONEY AND FIVE-SPICE PORK CHOPS

These chops take minimal effort to prepare and cook but the end result is delicious. Pork goes so well with these flavours – a match made in heaven.

SERVES 4 | PREP 15 MINS | COOK 20 MINS

- 2 TEASPOONS HONEY
- 2 TEASPOONS SOY SAUCE
- 1 TEASPOON CHINESE FIVE-SPICE POWDER
- ½ TEASPOON GARLIC POWDER
- 4 PORK CHOPS
- BROWN RICE AND SALAD, TO SERVE

Preheat the oven to 180°C, 160°C Fan, Gas Mark 4.

Mix the honey, soy sauce, five-spice and garlic powder together in a bowl and marinate the pork chops in this mixture for 10–15 minutes.

Place the pork chops in an ovenproof skillet or on a baking tray, empty any remaining marinade on top of them and bake for 20 minutes.

Serve with brown rice and salad.

TIP If you can, buy bone-in pork chops – they are cheaper and the bone adds more flavour. You also get the extra meat nestled around the bone that is stripped away when the bone is removed. Win-win.

CREAMY CHICKEN SPEEDY STEW

Another insanely easy dish that's so moreish it's unbelievable. It's a one-pot wonder too, which is always good for days when you want to eat fast but eat well.

SERVES 4 · PREP 5 MINS · COOK 40 MINS · BATCH

1 LARGE RED ONION, FINELY CHOPPED

3 GARLIC CLOVES, FINELY CHOPPED

OLIVE OIL

2 X 400G CANS OF CANNELLINI BEANS, 1 DRAINED, 1 WITH LIQUID RETAINED

4 CHICKEN BREASTS, DICED

200ML VEGETABLE STOCK

1 TABLESPOON GRATED PARMESAN CHEESE

1 TEASPOON MIXED FRESH HERBS

SALT, TO TASTE

COOKED GREENS OR SALAD, TO SERVE

In a pan, sauté the onion and garlic in a little olive oil, along with a good pinch of salt, until the onion has softened.

Add the beans, including the retained liquid. Simmer for 7–8 minutes, stirring often.

Add the chicken and the vegetable stock. Allow to simmer for around 20 minutes, stirring regularly. Add a little water if it starts to dry up. At the point where the sauce has thickened to a delicious creamy texture and the chicken has cooked, take off the heat.

Add the grated Parmesan and mixed herbs and stir well.

Serve with cooked greens or a salad.

BUTTERNUT SQUASH, RED LENTIL AND WHITE BEAN STEW

This is a wonderful dish for the colder months and freezes like a dream. Super simple and super cheap. It's also incredibly good for you, being high in fibre, B vitamins, antioxidants and protein.

SERVES 4 | PREP 5 MINS | COOK 25 MINS | BATCH

1 LARGE RED ONION, FINELY CHOPPED

2 GARLIC CLOVES, FINELY CHOPPED

OLIVE OIL

1 SMALL BUTTERNUT SQUASH, SKIN ON, DICED

180G DRY RED LENTILS

600ML VEGETABLE STOCK

1 X 400G CAN OF BUTTER BEANS, DRAINED

2 HANDFULS OF BABY SPINACH

SALT, TO TASTE

In a pan, sauté the onion and garlic in a little olive oil, along with a good pinch of salt, until the onion has softened.

Add the butternut squash and the lentils and enough stock to just cover everything in the pan.

Simmer for around 20–25 minutes, stirring frequently, until the lentils have almost completely broken down and created a thick stew and the squash is soft. You may need to add additional stock through the cooking process. You should end up with a porridge-like texture.

Add the butter beans and then the baby spinach and allow it to wilt before serving.

ONE-POT CHICKEN CURRY

This gorgeous dish is a double whammy – it's a perfect dish to batch cook and it's also a one-pot wonder so pretty hassle free. You can't get better. So, although this recipe serves 4, you can times it by as many as you like, depending on how many batches you want to make.

SERVES 4

PREP 5 MINS

COOK 45 MINS

BATCH

2 LARGE RED ONIONS, FINELY CHOPPED

5 GARLIC CLOVES, FINELY CHOPPED

OLIVE OIL

4 TABLESPOONS MADRAS OR BALTI CURRY PASTE

250G DRY RED LENTILS

1.3 LITRES VEGETABLE STOCK

4 CHICKEN BREASTS, DICED

SMALL HANDFUL OF FRESH CORIANDER, COARSELY TORN

SALT

In a pan, sauté the onions and garlic in a little olive oil, along with a good pinch of salt, until the onions have softened.

Add the curry paste and stir for around a minute, until the spices in the paste become more aromatic.

Add the lentils and a little of the vegetable stock. Keep adding the stock little and often, stirring frequently in a similar way to cooking a risotto, for 20–25 minutes until the lentils are cooked (soft and starting to fall apart). When you notice the liquid reducing, add a little more, and so on.

Add the diced chicken breasts, and keep simmering away for a further 15 minutes until the chicken is cooked.

Scatter over the coriander just before serving.

REPLACE AND SAVE
Average cost of takeaway chicken curry x 4 = £26
Average cost of Dale's chicken curry x 4 = £6.50

Total Family Saving: £19.50

TURKEY MEATBALLS

These are a great thing to stockpile the freezer with. You can make boxes of them and simply take a few out to add to pasta, have with a salad or even have in a sandwich – yep, really! Super easy and delicious. They can be shaped into burgers too that are great for the barbecue.

MAKES 20 BALLS · PREP 10 MINS · COOK 8 MINS · BATCH

1 LARGE RED ONION, FINELY CHOPPED

3 GARLIC CLOVES, FINELY CHOPPED

10 SUN-DRIED TOMATOES, FINELY CHOPPED

500G TURKEY MINCE

2 TEASPOONS DRIED MIXED HERBS

SALT AND PEPPER, TO TASTE

Place all the ingredients in a bowl, roll up your sleeves and get your hands in. Squidge and knead everything together, until thoroughly mixed.

Roll the mixture into balls about half the size of a golf ball. Gently lay them side by side in a plastic container that goes in the freezer. If it is deep enough to support another layer, place a sheet of greaseproof paper on top and start again. Whatever works.

Freeze the meatballs raw and just take out and cook what you need when you need it.

To cook, make sure the meatballs are thoroughly defrosted, heat a little olive oil in a pan and gently fry for 8–10 minutes until golden.

TIP Add breadcrumbs, made from leftover stale bread, to bulk up your meatballs and make the most out of your turkey mince.

FAMILY FAVOURITES WITH A FACELIFT

CHAPTER 4

TIPS FOR FUSSY EATERS

Fussy eaters can be a real struggle for families, from children refusing anything remotely healthy, through to everyone in the family eating different things at the same mealtime. Whilst it often takes time and patience to get these issues ironed out, here are a few tips that can help along the way.

1. GET THE KIDS INVOLVED

One of the best ways to get children more open to trying new foods and for breaking down barriers is to actually get them involved with the preparation of the meal. When they get involved they become emotionally invested in the creative process. Many studies have shown that this emotional investment makes children much more open and willing to eat the food, and can sometimes overcome the barrier of previously 'disliked' foods.

2. GET CREATIVE WITH TEXTURES, SHAPES, AND FLAVOURS

Sometimes it is the way a food is prepared and served that is the problem, and not the food itself. I love healthy food, but I still find it hard to get excited about a plate of steamed broccoli. Take that broccoli and stir-fry it with some garlic and chilli, now you're talking. So let's apply the same thinking to our family meals. If there is a problem food, how can you change it from the way you have served it before. Keeping with broccoli – how about blended into a soup? How about cut into tiny pieces and thrown into a curry? How about using it to make a pesto for pasta? Playing around with textures and flavours can be the key to breaking down that resistance to certain ingredients.

3. REINVENT OLD FAVOURITES

The biggest tip of all, and what this whole chapter focuses on, is just upgrading the foods that the family are prepared to eat. Start at this point and look for ways that you can up the nutritional density. Whether that is with ingredient swaps or adding in more veg, giving your favourites a facelift can be a key to getting more diversity of foods into peoples diets without major drama or rigmarole.

4. DUPING

OK, so this isn't necessarily my favourite tactic as I prefer to get children to openly enjoy new foods, but for those super tricky customers, getting just as tricky with them can sometimes be the only way to break through. This is especially good for kids who say they don't like a certain food or ingredient, when you know full well they have never tried it. Hiding these ingredients in a dish can open doors. If they like the dish, you can tell them that they have just eaten the food that they 'hate' and prove to them that there are ways they can actually enjoy the food in question. The Hidden Veg Tomato Sauce recipe in this chapter (see page 112) is a great example of this.

REPLACE AND SAVE

Save money by making your own versions of your favourite takeaways:
Dale's chicken kebab compared to takeaway kebab x 4 = family saving of £10
Dale's chicken tikka masala compared to takeaway x 4 = family saving of £22
Dale's pitta pizza compared to takeaway pizza x 4 = family saving of £9.49

Total Family Saving: £41.49

HIDDEN VEG TOMATO SAUCE

I'm generally not that in favour of 'hiding' fruit and veg in food or duping children into eating it. I prefer to try and find ways to inspire them and improve their relationship with such ingredients. However, best intentions aside, I have to admit there are some people out there that just won't eat any form of vegetation without a riot. This recipe, and the idea behind it, is for them. It can also be for those that just want to find as many creative ways as possible to make their food more nutritious. It makes a great pasta or pizza sauce and it's the base for quite a few dishes in this book, so it's worth making some batches up. It freezes beautifully.

MAKES 1 PORTION | PREP 5 MINS | COOK 20 MINS | BATCH

1 LARGE RED ONION, FINELY CHOPPED

2 GARLIC CLOVES, FINELY CHOPPED

OLIVE OIL

1 RED PEPPER, DESEEDED AND DICED

1 COURGETTE, DICED

500G TOMATO PASSATA

2 LARGE HANDFULS OF BABY SPINACH

SALT, TO TASTE

In a pan, sauté the onion and garlic in a little olive oil, along with a good pinch of salt, until the onion has softened.

Add the pepper and courgette and continue to cook until they begin to soften. Add the passata and simmer for 10–12 minutes, until all the vegetables are soft.

Add the spinach and turn off the heat. There will be enough heat in the sauce to wilt the spinach.

Transfer all of this to a blender and then whizz into a sauce that looks, smells and tastes just like a regular tomato sauce, yet has an abundance of nutrients packed in.

REPLACE AND SAVE
You could always use frozen spinach here instead of fresh to make it even cheaper. You can get 5 times the amount of frozen spinach for the same price.
1kg frozen spinach = £1.50
200g fresh baby leaf spinach = £1.50

PIMPED-UP LASAGNE

Now, this is family comfort food at the highest level. Few things beat a good lasagne. This version really hits the spot – and it has a nutritional boost. We use the Hidden Veg Tomato Sauce here, and adding lentils to the mix gives extra fibre, protein and B vitamins.

SERVES 4 | PREP 10 MINS | COOK 1 HOUR

180G DRY RED LENTILS

500G LEAN MINCED BEEF

OLIVE OIL

1 PORTION OF HIDDEN VEG TOMATO SAUCE (SEE PAGE 112)

250G LASAGNE SHEETS

50G SOFT CHEESE

¼ TEASPOON NUTMEG

SPRINKLE OF GRATED MATURE CHEDDAR

SALT, TO TASTE

SALAD, TO SERVE

Preheat the oven to 200°C, 180°C Fan, Gas Mark 6.

Place the lentils in a saucepan and cover with boiling water. Simmer until they're about two-thirds cooked – the edges should be soft and the middles still firm. This should take about 10 minutes. Drain and set aside.

Place the mince in the saucepan with a little olive oil and gently fry for 7–8 minutes, until it's almost cooked through.

Add the lentils and the hidden veg sauce. Cook for about 10 minutes until the mixture has thickened and become a rich ragout.

Place a thin layer of the ragout in the bottom of a baking dish, add a layer of lasagne, then a layer of ragout, then a layer of lasagne and repeat until you've almost filled the dish.

Mix the soft cheese with a small amount of water to create a cream-like texture. Add the nutmeg and a pinch of salt, then pour over the top of the lasagne. Sprinkle over the Cheddar.

Bake for 30 minutes until everything is bubbling, the lasagne sheets are cooked through and the top is golden brown.

Serve with a salad.

FALLON'S CHICKEN CURRY

In series one of the show, we created a curry that was a real hit and it highlighted perfectly how you can still enjoy your favourite dish, but by modifying the recipe you can create a far healthier version. Making the sauce with velvety sweet potato is a great technique for getting veg into fussy eaters.

SERVES 4 · PREP 10 MINS · COOK 45 MINS · BATCH

1 RED ONION, FINELY CHOPPED

3 GARLIC CLOVES, FINELY CHOPPED

OLIVE OIL

1–2 SWEET POTATOES, PEELED AND DICED

500ML VEGETABLE STOCK

MILD CURRY POWDER

4 SKINLESS CHICKEN BREASTS, DICED

ANY ADDITIONAL VEGETABLES (BABY SPINACH, PEAS, MUSHROOMS, ETC.), OPTIONAL

HANDFUL OF FRESH CORIANDER, COARSELY TORN

SALT AND PEPPER, TO TASTE

BROWN RICE, TO SERVE

Sauté the onion and garlic in a little olive oil, along with a good pinch of salt, until the onion has softened.

Add the diced sweet potatoes and enough vegetable stock to just cover them.

Simmer for 15 minutes until the sweet potatoes have softened. At this point season and add enough curry powder to achieve a taste that you like. I recommend starting with 1 tablespoon and then working from there.

Transfer to a blender or use a stick blender, and whizz into a smooth purée. Aim for a texture like a thick soup. Taste the sauce. If it needs more seasoning or more curry powder, now is the time to add it.

Return the sauce to the pan. Add the diced chicken, then simmer over a medium heat for around 20 minutes, until the chicken is cooked. Stir frequently, ensuring no sticking on the base of the pan.

At this stage you could add some baby spinach, peas, mushrooms or any additional veg, and cook for another 4–5 minutes before serving. If you don't want to, that's all good, this is still a nutrient-rich dish.

Sprinkle over the coriander before serving with brown rice.

VEGGIE FRIED NOODLES

Who doesn't love noodles? Just look at the queues at the well-known noodle outlets on a weekend and you can see that families love 'em! It is insanely simple to make this type of dish at home and you can load it up with all sorts.

SERVES 4
PREP 10 MINS
COOK 20 MINS

300G NOODLES
(UDON, EGG NOODLES, ETC.)

1 LARGE RED ONION,
HALVED THEN SLICED

4 GARLIC CLOVES, FINELY CHOPPED

1 COURGETTE, CUT
INTO MATCHSTICKS

1 RED PEPPER, DESEEDED
AND CUT LENGTHWAYS

OLIVE OIL

100G CHESTNUT MUSHROOMS

4 SPRING ONIONS, CUT LENGTHWAYS

2 TABLESPOONS SOY SAUCE

1 TABLESPOON SESAME OIL

2 LARGE EGGS

Cook the noodles according to the packet instructions. Drain and set aside.

In a wok or pan, stir-fry the onion, garlic, courgette and pepper in a little olive oil until they begin to soften.

Add the mushrooms and spring onions and continue to cook for 2–3 minutes. Add the cooked noodles. Add the soy sauce and the sesame oil and mix everything together well.

In a separate pan, crack the eggs and loosely whisk as if you were cooking scrambled egg. Mix the egg in with the noodles before serving.

REPLACE AND SAVE
Average cost of takeaway veggie noodles x 4 = £22
Average cost of Dale's veggie noodles x 4 = £5

Total Family Saving: £17

FISH FINGERS AND CHIPS
(BUT NOT AS WE KNOW IT)

There is no denying that fish fingers and chips is a family teatime institution. This version greatly boosts your omega-3 fatty acid intake and gives you a healthy dose of the antioxidant beta-carotene and fibre too!

SERVES 4 | PREP 5 MINS | COOK 35 MINS

4 SKINLESS SALMON FILLETS

2 EGGS, BEATEN

OATMEAL

2 LARGE SWEET POTATOES, SKIN ON, CUT INTO WEDGES

OLIVE OIL

PEAS OR COOKED GREENS, TO SERVE

Preheat the oven to 180°C, 160°C Fan, Gas Mark 4.

Cut the salmon fillets into fingers. Dip each salmon finger into the beaten egg, then roll in the oatmeal.

Place the salmon on a baking sheet and bake for 25–30 minutes, until golden brown with a crunchy coating.

Place the sweet potato wedges on another baking sheet, drizzle with olive oil and toss well. Bake for around 20–25 minutes until soft with crispy edges.

Serve with peas or any cooked greens.

BOOSTED BOLOGNESE

Spag bol. A real family favourite up and down the country – and one that can be a monumental calorie bomb if we aren't careful. This version created for the Smith family in the first series of the show went down an absolute storm. The changes aren't huge – just a couple of tweaks and this dish becomes so much better for you. By swapping white pasta for brown we up the fibre, and adding the lentils means extra protein, fibre and B vitamins.

SERVES 4 · PREP 5 MINS · COOK 35 MINS · BATCH

180G DRY RED LENTILS

1 LARGE RED ONION, FINELY CHOPPED

2 GARLIC CLOVES, FINELY CHOPPED

1 RED PEPPER, DESEEDED AND FINELY CHOPPED

OLIVE OIL

500G LEAN MINCED BEEF

1 TABLESPOON TOMATO PURÉE

2 X 400G CANS OF CHOPPED TOMATOES

250ML BEEF STOCK

300G WHOLEWHEAT SPAGHETTI

HANDFUL OF BASIL LEAVES

SALT, TO TASTE

MIXED LEAF SALAD, TO SERVE

Place the lentils in a saucepan, cover with boiling water and simmer for 15–20 until soft, then drain and set aside.

Meanwhile, in a pan, sauté the onion, garlic and red pepper in a little olive oil, along with a pinch of salt, until the onion and pepper have softened.

Add the mince and gently fry for 7–8 minutes, until it's cooked through. Stir in the tomato purée. Add the lentils, chopped tomatoes and stock and simmer for 10–15 minutes, until the sauce has thickened.

Finally, cook the spaghetti until al dente or according to the packet instructions.

Scatter over the basil leaves before serving with a mixed leaf salad.

TIPS Try to reduce the portion size of the spaghetti and fill up on the beautiful bolognese. You can batch cook the bolognese – it freezes well and can be used for other dishes such as cottage pie and lasagne.

BURGERS TWO WAYS

Burgers are often seen as super unhealthy. This really needn't be the case though. When you make them yourself you can control what's in them, and actually they are just minced meat with whatever flavours you add. Simple, wholesome food. Here are two versions for some variety.

SERVES 4 | PREP 70 MINS | COOK 20 MINS

FOR THE BEEF BURGERS

500G LEAN MINCED BEEF

¼ RED ONION, FINELY CHOPPED

1 GARLIC CLOVE, FINELY CHOPPED

4–5 SUN-DRIED TOMATOES, FINELY CHOPPED

FOR THE THAI CHICKEN BURGERS

500G MINCED CHICKEN BREAST

SMALL BUNCH OF FRESH CORIANDER, ROUGHLY CHOPPED

2 TABLESPOONS THAI RED CURRY PASTE

SEEDED BUNS, LETTUCE, SLICED TOMATO AND SLICED ONION, TO SERVE

The method for both burgers is exactly the same.

Place the minced meat into a large bowl. Add the flavour components and then roll up your sleeves and squidge everything together with your hands until it is well mixed.

Form into 4 burger patties and place on a plate.

Chill in the fridge for an hour or so before cooking to firm them up.

These burgers can be oven baked, fried or put on the barbecue. Cooking time is 20 minutes in the oven at 180°C, 160°C Fan, Gas Mark 4, or fry or barbecue for 15 minutes. All cooking methods require turning occasionally.

Serve in seeded buns with lettuce, sliced tomato and sliced onion.

REPLACE AND SAVE
Average cost of chain restaurant burger x 4 – £36
Average cost of Dale's burger x 4 – £12
Total Family Saving: £24

SWEET POTATO COTTAGE PIE

Cottage pie is one of those family staples that pleases every generation.
Hearty, homely and warming, it has the ultimate feel-good factor.
This version takes the classic comfort food and gives it a nutritional
upgrade for good measure. Simple changes with big benefits.

SERVES 4
PREP 5 MINS
COOK 75 MINS

4 SWEET POTATOES,
PEELED AND DICED

1 LARGE RED ONION,
FINELY CHOPPED

3 GARLIC CLOVES, FINELY CHOPPED

OLIVE OIL

500G LEAN MINCED BEEF

400G TOMATO PASSATA

2 TEASPOONS STOCK POWDER

SALT AND PEPPER, TO TASTE

COOKED GREENS OR SALAD,
TO SERVE

Preheat the oven to 180°C, 160°C Fan, Gas Mark 4.

Place the sweet potatoes in a pan, top with boiling water and simmer for 15 minutes until soft. Drain and set aside.

In a pan, sauté the onion and garlic in a little olive oil, along with a good pinch of salt, until the onion has softened.

Add the beef mince and gently fry for 7–8 minutes, until the mince is almost cooked. Add the passata and stock powder and allow to reduce for around 15 minutes, until you get a thick, rich, meaty filling. Keep stirring regularly so it doesn't stick. Set aside.

Mash the sweet potatoes and season with a little salt and pepper.

Place the filling in an oven dish, and then top with the sweet potato mash. Pat the potato down well to make a sealed lid over the meat. Run a fork across the top of the potato mash – this creates a lovely crunch as the grooves crisp up.

Place in the oven for around 30 minutes, until a golden crust has formed.

Serve with cooked greens or a salad.

THE PITTA PIZZA

This simple dish is an amazing hack. So many families spend a fortune on takeaway pizzas. And let's not fool ourselves, most of the takeaway pizzas around tend to be incredibly unhealthy – massively high in nasty fats and refined carbohydrates, and the calories per serving will make the mind boggle. This version will save you all that bad stuff, save you a heap of money and will give you a nutrient boost. Bargain!

SERVES 1 | **PREP** 10 MINS | **COOK** 5 MINS

HANDFUL OF BABY SPINACH

2–3 TEASPOONS TOMATO PURÉE

1 LARGE WHOLEMEAL PITTA BREAD

½ GARLIC CLOVE, FINELY CHOPPED

4–5 CHERRY TOMATOES, HALVED

50G FETA CHEESE

4 BLACK OLIVES, PITTED

HANDFUL OF FRESH MINT LEAVES, COARSELY TORN

SALT AND PEPPER, TO TASTE

Begin by wilting the spinach. Place it in a pan with about 2 tablespoons of boiled water. Place over high heat so that the water simmers. Cover and cook for 3–4 minutes – it will wilt very quickly. Remove from the heat, drain any liquid and leave to cool for a few moments. Once cool enough to handle, give it a gentle squeeze to get rid of any excess water.

Preheat the grill.

Spread the tomato purée evenly over the pitta bread. Add the chopped garlic, wilted spinach and cherry tomatoes, then crumble over the feta. Season with salt and pepper and top with the olives.

Place under the hot grill for about 5 minutes or until the cheese begins to turn golden brown at the edges.

Scatter over the mint leaves before serving immediately.

REPLACE AND SAVE
Average cost of pitta pizzas x 4 = £7.50
Average cost of a family-size takeaway pizza = £16.99
Total Family Saving: £9.49

CHICKEN TIKKA MASALA

One of Britain's favourite dishes! A takeaway chicken tikka masala is a tasty treat for sure, but if you want a healthy *and* tasty version, this is it.

SERVES 4

PREP 5 MINS

COOK 30 MINS

BATCH

1 LARGE RED ONION, FINELY CHOPPED

4 GARLIC CLOVES, FINELY CHOPPED

1 CINNAMON STICK

1 STAR ANISE

OLIVE OIL

100G TIKKA MASALA PASTE

400G TOMATO PASSATA

1 X 400ML CAN OF COCONUT MILK

4 CHICKEN BREASTS, DICED

HANDFUL OF FRESH CORIANDER, COARSELY TORN

SALT, TO TASTE

BROWN RICE, TO SERVE

In a pan, sauté the onion, garlic, cinnamon and star anise in a little olive oil, along with a good pinch of salt, until the onion begins to soften and the spices are aromatic.

Add the tikka masala paste and sauté for another 2 minutes.

Add the passata and coconut milk along with the diced chicken and simmer for 15–20 minutes, stirring often, until the sauce has thickened and all the flavours have matured.

Scatter over the fresh coriander before serving with brown rice.

REPLACE AND SAVE

This recipe is great if you are trying to lose weight.
Average fat content in a takeaway chicken tikka masala = 40g per portion
Average fat content in Dale's chicken tikka masala = 5g per portion

Total Fat Content Saving: 35g per portion

CHILLI CON CARNE

Chilli con carne isn't that unhealthy as dishes go, but some of the ready-made ones can have quite a high sugar content, which is why we were asked for a recipe for this family favourite. We also think every mealtime is an opportunity to get the good stuff in so of course we opted for the high-fibre upgrade – mixed beans.

SERVES 4 | PREP 5 MINS | COOK 35 MINS | BATCH

1 RED ONION, FINELY CHOPPED

2–3 GARLIC CLOVES, FINELY CHOPPED

2 GREEN CHILLIES, FINELY CHOPPED

OLIVE OIL

300G LEAN MINCED BEEF

1 TABLESPOON TOMATO PURÉE

1 X 400G CAN OF MIXED BEANS, DRAINED

2 X 400G CANS OF CHOPPED TOMATOES

200ML BEEF STOCK

1 TEASPOON SMOKED PAPRIKA

1 TEASPOON GROUND CUMIN

HANDFUL OF FRESH CORIANDER, COARSELY TORN

SALT, TO TASTE

BROWN RICE, TO SERVE

In a pan, sauté the onion, garlic and chillies in a little olive oil, along with a good pinch of salt, until the onion has softened.

Add the mince and brown for 7–8 minutes before adding the tomato purée, beans, chopped tomatoes, stock, paprika and cumin.

Simmer for 20 minutes to allow the sauce to reduce down and become thick and rich. This stage is really worth it as the flavours will mature beautifully.

At this point, taste the dish. You could add more paprika and cumin if you think it needs it.

Scatter over the fresh coriander before serving with brown rice.

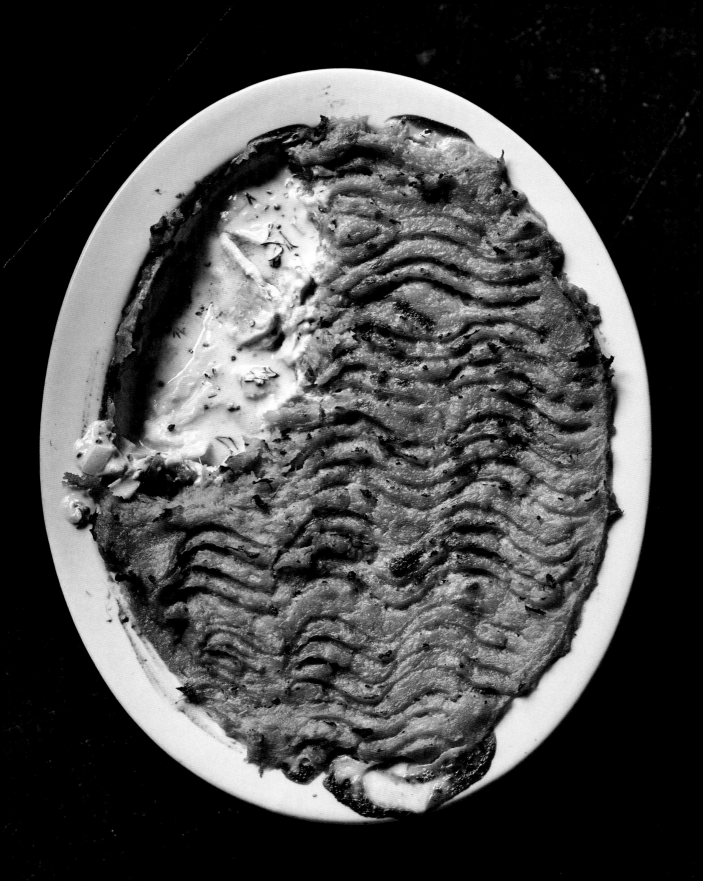

THE BEST FISH PIE EVER

Fish pie is another of those absolute feel-good home favourites. Flavoursome, hearty, creamy. What's not to love? Well, the traditional one based on a roux can be incredibly rich and contain a lot of refined carbohydrates. This version is lighter and much more nutrient dense.

SERVES 4 | PREP 10 MINS | COOK 60 MINS

4 SWEET POTATOES, PEELED AND DICED

2 WHITE ONIONS, FINELY CHOPPED

3 GARLIC CLOVES, FINELY CHOPPED

OLIVE OIL

500G LOW-FAT SOFT CHEESE

400ML VEGETABLE STOCK

5 TEASPOONS WHOLEGRAIN MUSTARD

800G FISH PIE MIX

20G DILL, ROUGHLY CHOPPED

SALT AND PEPPER

COOKED GREENS OR SALAD, TO SERVE

Preheat the oven to 200°C, 180°C Fan, Gas Mark 6.

Place the sweet potatoes in a saucepan, cover with boiling water and simmer for around 20 minutes, until very soft. Drain then mash, season with salt and pepper, and set aside.

In a pan, sauté the onions and garlic in a little olive oil, along with a pinch of salt, until the onions have softened.

Add the soft cheese, stock and mustard to the pan and stir well over a medium heat. Add the fish pie mix and simmer for 10 minutes, until the fish is almost cooked. Stir through the dill.

Transfer the mixture to an oven dish. Top with the sweet potato mash and place in the oven on a high shelf. Bake for about 15 minutes, or until the sauce is bubbling at the sides and the mash is starting to get crispy.

Serve with cooked greens or a salad.

SPINACH AND SWEET POTATO CURRY

This dish is a true winner. It is a great beginner curry – one for people that have never cooked a curry from scratch and feel a little nervous about doing so. This proved a popular hit after I showed it on *Eat, Shop, Save* to Ellouise and Jamie, who stockpiled their freezer with this gorgeous dish. You can add prawns or other seafood at the end if you like to make different varieties.

SERVES 4 | PREP 10 MINS | COOK 35 MINS | BATCH

2 RED ONIONS, THINLY SLICED

2 GARLIC CLOVES, FINELY CHOPPED

1 TEASPOON GRATED FRESH ROOT GINGER

2 GREEN CHILLIES, THINLY SLICED

OLIVE OIL

1 TEASPOON GROUND CORIANDER

1 TEASPOON GROUND CUMIN

1 TEASPOON BLACK MUSTARD SEEDS

1 HEAPED TEASPOON TURMERIC

4 SWEET POTATOES (ABOUT 800G), SKIN ON, CUT INTO SMALL WEDGES

800ML VEGETABLE STOCK

2 LARGE HANDFULS OF SPINACH, COARSELY CHOPPED

LARGE HANDFUL OF FRESH CORIANDER, COARSELY TORN

In a large saucepan, sauté the onions, garlic, ginger and chillies in a little olive oil until the onions have softened. Add all the spices and cook for 1–2 minutes, until they have become fragrant.

Add the sweet potatoes and stock and simmer for about 15–20 minutes until the sweet potatoes are soft. To start with the curry will look like an ugly vegetable stew, but after this time simmering, two things will happen. The liquid will evaporate and reduce in volume and the starch will leach out of the sweet potato into the remaining liquid, creating a thick sauce.

At this point add the spinach. Once the spinach has wilted, add the fresh coriander.

CHICKEN TRAY BAKE

Tray bakes have become popular over the last few years, with many of those bake-in-the-bag packet mixes appearing on the market. This is the same principle but I guarantee it tastes a million times better.

2 LARGE RED ONIONS, CUT INTO 16 WEDGES

3 GARLIC CLOVES, FINELY CHOPPED

1 RED PEPPER, DESEEDED AND CUT LENGTHWAYS

1 GREEN PEPPER, DESEEDED AND CUT LENGTHWAYS

2 TABLESPOONS OLIVE OIL

2 TABLESPOONS BALSAMIC VINEGAR

1 TEASPOON DRIED MIXED HERBS

4 CHICKEN LEGS

2 TABLESPOONS BLACK OLIVES, PITTED

SALT, TO TASTE

Preheat the oven to 180°C, 160°C Fan, Gas Mark 4.

Place the onions, garlic and peppers in a roasting tin. Add the olive oil, balsamic vinegar and dried herbs, along with a pinch of salt, and mix everything together well.

Place the chicken legs on top of the vegetables and place in the oven for about 30 minutes.

After 15 minutes, take the tray out, remove the chicken, stir the vegetables well, place the chicken back on top and return the tray to the oven for the remaining 15 minutes.

CROWD-PLEASING STIR-FRY

Stir-fries often find themselves on the family favourites list but,
I beg you, please stay away from the sugar-laden, over-processed,
pre-made sauces. Learn how to create this simple staple from
scratch. Building up these basic flavours will make a dish that tastes
far superior, costs less and is much better for you. This recipe uses
chicken but you can keep it veg, or swap the chicken for tofu,
prawns or beef. All work beautifully with these flavours.

SERVES 4 · **PREP 10 MINS** · **COOK 30 MINS**

1 LARGE RED ONION, THINLY SLICED

4 GARLIC CLOVES, FINELY CHOPPED

OLIVE OIL

1 COURGETTE, CUT INTO
HALF CIRCLES

1 RED PEPPER, DESEEDED
AND SLICED LENGTHWAYS

150G CHESTNUT MUSHROOMS,
SLICED

4 CHICKEN BREASTS, DICED

250G GREENS, SHREDDED

2 TABLESPOONS SOY SAUCE

1 TABLESPOON TOASTED SESAME OIL

2 TEASPOONS HONEY

1 TEASPOON CHINESE
FIVE-SPICE POWDER

1 TEASPOON CORNFLOUR

150ML WATER

SALT, TO TASTE

BROWN RICE, TO SERVE

In a large saucepan or wok, stir-fry the onion and
garlic in a little olive oil, along with a good pinch
of salt, until the onion has softened.

Add the courgette and pepper and continue to cook
until they begin to soften.

Add the mushrooms and diced chicken and stir-fry
for 10–12 minutes, until the chicken is cooked.

Add the greens and stir-fry until they have softened.
Add the soy sauce, sesame oil, honey and five-spice
and mix well.

Add the cornflour to the water and mix together. Pour
this mixture into the pan and stir well – it will magically
thicken almost instantly, creating a thick, smooth sauce
to coat all of the ingredients.

Serve with brown rice.

SAUSAGE AND CHICKPEA HOTPOT

This takes the classic sausage casserole and turns it on its head.
Including chickpeas here hugely ramps up the fibre and the B vitamins.
Making this on the stovetop makes it cook a little faster.

SERVES 4 · PREP 5 MINS · COOK 30 MINS · BATCH

1 LARGE RED ONION, FINELY CHOPPED

2 GARLIC CLOVES, FINELY CHOPPED

2–3 ROSEMARY SPRIGS

OLIVE OIL

8 SAUSAGES

1 X 400G CAN OF CHICKPEAS, DRAINED

400G TOMATO PASSATA

1 TEASPOON SMOKED PAPRIKA

SALT, TO TASTE

SWEET POTATO MASH, TO SERVE

In a pan, sauté the onion, garlic and rosemary in a little olive oil, along with a good pinch of salt, until the onion has softened.

Add the sausages and brown for about a minute, stirring often.

Add the chickpeas, passata and paprika and simmer for around 20 minutes, until the sausages are fully cooked, the sauce has thickened and the flavours have intensified.

Serve with sweet potato mash.

REPLACE AND SAVE
Average cost of a hotpot ready meal x 4 = £10
Average cost of Dale's hotpot x 4 = £5.40

Total Family Saving: £4.60

TUNA PASTA BAKE

This glorious dish is one of those crowd-pleasers that kids, fussy eaters and comfort-food lovers all unite on. This version takes this delicious classic and ramps it up nutritionally without even remotely skimping on taste. You can add additional veg if you like. I often add a couple of extra handfuls of spinach to the sauce and wilt it down. But don't worry if not, as it already has plenty.

SERVES 4 | PREP 5 MINS | COOK 30 MINS

300G WHOLEWHEAT PASTA

170G TINNED TUNA, DRAINED

1 PORTION OF HIDDEN VEG TOMATO SAUCE (*SEE* PAGE 112)

100G EXTRA MATURE CHEDDAR CHEESE, GRATED

SALAD, TO SERVE

Preheat the oven to 180°C, 160°C Fan, Gas Mark 4.

Place the pasta in a saucepan and cover with boiling water. Cook until al dente or according to the packet instructions. Drain and set aside.

Place the tuna in a separate saucepan and add in the sauce. Stir well, making sure the tuna is flaked and mixed through the sauce.

Add the cooked pasta to the sauce and mix well. Transfer to a baking dish and top with the cheese. Bake for about 15–20 minutes, long enough for the cheese to melt and the edges to crisp up a little.

Serve with a salad.

SOUPS

CHAPTER

5

TIPS FOR EXERCISING, DRINKING & SNACKING SMART

 ## SNACK SMART

HOMEMADE POPCORN

Not the more expensive, pre-made, shop-bought stuff which is often loaded with salt and sugar. Instead, make your own. You can personalize it with your favourite flavours, it's fun for the kids, and it's much healthier than snacking on crisps!

STEVE'S STICKY BARS

This healthy take on the flapjack is a brilliant way to combat sugar cravings and therefore lose weight. Cook a batch to take to work with you so you can easily avoid mid-afternoon temptation!

HUMMUS AND CRUDITÉS

Try chopping up carrots, celery and red peppers into sticks and dipping them in hummus as a healthy snack that is full of protein and nutrients to get you through the day. You can make batches of the hummus recipe on page 47. For a handy snack on the go, why not get an empty jar, put some hummus in the bottom, add the crudités on top, then put the lid on ready to crack the jar open when you need it!

HEALTHY CRACKERS WITH HEALTHY TOPPINGS

Healthy crackers are easy to buy from the supermarket – look out for ones that are savoury and high in fibre. The ideas for toppings are endless. Why not try low-fat cream cheese and chopped grapes, peanut butter, or even chopped tomatoes. Get creative!

PEANUT BUTTER AND APPLE

Cut an apple into slices and dip them into peanut butter.

NUTS

Nuts are incredibly rich in good fats, protein and nutrients. They are so nutrient-rich that you only need a few to keep you going. A small handful should do it!

FRUIT

Fruit is always a good snack idea. Berries, apples, tangerines and bananas are all great options.

EXERCISE SMART

BE REALISTIC

If you've tended to shy away from exercise in the past, know that you're not going to run a marathon straight away! Be realistic with your goals. Start with a 15 minute brisk walk and build up from there.

GET MOVING

Exercise doesn't have to be about sweating it out for hours in the gym. Even small changes such as walking up the escalator instead of standing, or walking round the block in your lunch break can make a difference. Try to get as much movement into your day as you can.

BUDDY UP

Find a friend or family member to exercise with. You're much less likely to sack it off if someone else is holding you accountable. Plus, it's much more fun!

CLASS ACT

There are loads of options for classes nowadays, from Zumba to water aerobics to 80s-style dance with glow sticks! There are so many for you to try so find one that suits you. Lots of gyms allow a trial period so check out what your local gym has to offer. Flexible memberships such as Class Pass are also a brilliant way to see what's on in your area.

DRINK SMART

DRINK MORE WATER

Drinking lots of water has so many health benefits, and it can also help to curb your appetite if you're feeling hungry. Over the next 8 weeks, try drinking at least 8 cups of water a day, and see how you feel!

MAKE WATER MORE INTERESTING

If you get bored of plain old water, you can easily liven it up. Try adding lemon, lime or cucumber slices, or even frozen berries. Stay away from squash as it can often be high in sugar.

WATCH THE ALCOHOL

Alcohol is very high in calories. Even if you are eating healthily, if you drink a lot of alcohol you'll be undoing all that good work! Try to keep alcohol to a minimum.

NO MORE FIZZY DRINKS AND ENERGY DRINKS

They are loaded with sugar and can also be expensive. If you need a caffeine hit, a cup of black coffee is a healthier way to get it. You could also try herbal teas.

LENTIL AND BACON

This is an absolute classic. OK, bacon may not be top of the healthy ingredients list, but a little bit now and again is all good. The lentils on the other hand… They are awesome. Rich in soluble fibre and protein, they keep you feeling satisfied, don't pack much in terms of calories and are a great source of B vitamins.

SERVES 4 · PREP 5 MINS · COOK 30 MINS · BATCH

1 LARGE RED ONION, FINELY CHOPPED

2 GARLIC CLOVES, FINELY CHOPPED

OLIVE OIL

200G SMOKED BACON LARDONS

¼ TEASPOON TURMERIC

½ TEASPOON GROUND CORIANDER

250G DRY RED LENTILS

1.2L VEGETABLE STOCK

SALT AND PEPPER, TO TASTE

In a pan, sauté the onion and garlic in a little olive oil, along with a good pinch of salt, until the onion begins to soften.

Add the lardons and continue to sauté until they have cooked (around 3–4 minutes). Add the spices and mix well.

Add the lentils and a third of the stock. Allow to simmer until the stock reduces and the soup thickens (about 20 minutes), stirring frequently to avoid sticking. Add more stock, little and often, at this point, until the finished soup resembles a thin porridge.

TIP If you want to be healthier, substitute the bacon for some seasonal vegetables – a few handfuls of spinach leaves and diced tomato would work well here.

CREAMY GREEN SOUP

OK… give me a chance here. Don't be put off by the colour of this soup and the fact it contains green vegetables. This is absolutely delicious and kids actually love it!

SERVES 4 · PREP 5 MINS · COOK 20 MINS · BATCH

1 WHITE ONION, FINELY CHOPPED

1 GARLIC CLOVE, FINELY CHOPPED

OLIVE OIL

350G PEAS (FRESH OR FROZEN)

1 LARGE COURGETTE, ROUGHLY CHOPPED

1 LARGE POTATO, SKIN ON AND DICED

1 X 400ML CAN OF COCONUT MILK

500ML VEGETABLE STOCK

1 BAG OF BABY SPINACH

SALT, TO TASTE

In a pan, sauté the onion and garlic in a little olive oil, along with a pinch of salt, until the onion has softened.

Add the peas, keeping back a handful to add in at the end, the courgette, potato and coconut milk. Add enough vegetable stock to cover. Simmer for 10 minutes until the potato has softened.

Stir in the baby spinach a handful at a time, until it has all wilted.

Transfer to a blender, or use a stick blender, and blitz into a smooth soup.

Add the remaining peas before serving.

ROASTED SWEET POTATO, COCONUT AND WHITE BEAN

This is such a delicious soup. Smooth, rich, flavoursome and incredibly nutrient dense. Slow-release carbohydrates, healthy fats, fibre, protein… Who'd have thought something so simple could be such a powerhouse.

SERVES 4 | PREP 5 MINS | COOK 35 MINS | BATCH

2 SWEET POTATOES, SKIN ON, DICED

OLIVE OIL

1 LARGE RED ONION, FINELY CHOPPED

3 GARLIC CLOVES, FINELY CHOPPED

1 X 400ML CAN OF COCONUT MILK

1 X 400G CAN OF CANNELLINI BEANS, DRAINED

600–750ML VEGETABLE STOCK

SALT, TO TASTE

Preheat the oven to 180°C, 160°C Fan, Gas Mark 4.

Place the diced sweet potatoes on a baking tray and drizzle with a small amount of olive oil, 1 teaspoon max, and mix well. Roast for 30 minutes or until soft with golden brown edges.

Whilst the sweet potatoes are roasting, sauté the onion and garlic in a pan in a little olive oil, along with a good pinch of salt, until the onion has softened.

Once the potatoes are cooked, add to the pan with the onion and garlic.

Add the coconut milk, two-thirds of the beans and the vegetable stock. Simmer for 2–3 minutes.

Transfer to a blender, or use a stick blender, and whizz until smooth. Add the remaining beans just before serving so they are whole in the soup.

CURRIED PARSNIP

I adore this. It is cheap as chips, and the compounds that give parsnips their sweet flavour help to support the growth of good gut bacteria.

SERVES 4 · PREP 5 MINS · COOK 20 MINS · BATCH

1 LARGE WHITE ONION, FINELY CHOPPED

3 GARLIC CLOVES, FINELY CHOPPED

OLIVE OIL

4 LARGE PARSNIPS, SKIN ON, DICED

800ML VEGETABLE STOCK

1 TABLESPOON MILD CURRY POWDER

SALT, TO TASTE

Sauté the onion and garlic in a pan in a little olive oil, along with a good pinch of salt, until the onion has softened.

Add the diced parsnips and cover with the vegetable stock. Simmer for 10 minutes until the parsnip is soft and falls apart with a small amount of pressure from a fork.

Add the curry powder then transfer to a blender or use a stick blender and blitz into the smoothest, silkiest soup imaginable. If you need to add more liquid, top it up with a little water.

TOMATO AND RED PEPPER

This is one of the easiest soups you could ever imagine. Plus it's packed with antioxidants, vitamin C, beta-carotene and a whole host of other goodies.

SERVES 4 · PREP 5 MINS · COOK 20 MINS · BATCH

1 LARGE RED ONION, FINELY CHOPPED

2 GARLIC CLOVES, FINELY CHOPPED

OLIVE OIL

2 LARGE RED PEPPERS, DESEEDED AND DICED

1 X 400G CAN OF CHOPPED TOMATOES

500ML VEGETABLE STOCK

SALT, TO TASTE

In a pan, sauté the onion and garlic in a little olive oil, along with a good pinch of salt, until the onion has softened.

Add the diced peppers and continue to cook for 7–8 minutes until the peppers begin to soften. Pour in the chopped tomatoes and stock and simmer for 3–4 minutes.

Transfer to a blender, or use a stick blender, and blitz into a smooth soup.

THE WINTER WARMER

This one kicks like Bruce Lee! It's perfect for the colder months, or if you are feeling a little under the weather and need to clear your head. You can adjust the spice to taste, but the chilli hit works so well.

SERVES 4 | PREP 10 MINS | COOK 25 MINS | BATCH

1 LARGE RED ONION, FINELY CHOPPED

4 GARLIC CLOVES, FINELY CHOPPED

1 THUMB-SIZED PIECE OF FRESH ROOT GINGER, PEELED AND CHOPPED

1 FRESH THAI CHILLI, SEEDS IN, CHOPPED

OLIVE OIL

2 LARGE SWEET POTATOES, SKIN ON, DICED

2 TEASPOONS TURMERIC POWDER

1 TEASPOON CINNAMON POWDER

800ML VEGETABLE STOCK

SALT, TO TASTE

In a pan, sauté the onion, garlic, ginger and chilli in a little olive oil, along with a good pinch of salt, until the onion has softened.

Add the diced sweet potatoes and the turmeric and cinnamon powder, then cover with the vegetable stock. Simmer for 15 minutes until the potato is soft.

Transfer to a blender, or use a stick blender, and whizz until velvety smooth.

TIP Making your own vegetable stock is easy and great for using up leftover vegetables. It can be made in batches and frozen, and it is healthier too – shop-bought stock cubes are often high in sodium and may contain artificial ingredients.

BLACK BEAN SOUP

Ohhh this soup! There is something so comforting about it. Black beans have become really quite popular lately, and with good reason I say. They are very rich in a group of compounds called anthocyanins, which are responsible for their dark purple (not black at all, as it goes) colour pigment. These compounds are also found in red wine. They benefit heart health in several ways.

SERVES 4 · PREP 5 MINS · COOK 20 MINS · BATCH

1 LARGE WHITE ONION, FINELY CHOPPED

3 GARLIC CLOVES, FINELY CHOPPED

OLIVE OIL

2 X 400G CANS OF BLACK BEANS, 1 DRAINED, 1 WITH LIQUID RETAINED

1 LARGE POTATO, DICED

750ML VEGETABLE STOCK

1 TEASPOON GROUND CUMIN

1 TEASPOON GROUND CORIANDER

SALT, TO TASTE

In a pan, sauté the onion and garlic in a little olive oil, along with a good pinch of salt, until the onion has softened.

Add the black beans, including the retained liquid, saving 2 tablespoons of beans to add at the end. Add the diced potato and the vegetable stock and simmer for 10 minutes until the potato has softened. Add the spices.

Transfer to a blender, or use a stick blender, and blitz into a smooth soup.

Add the remaining black beans before serving to give a little texture.

RED CURRY SQUASH

This soup is serious! An absolute flavour explosion. This could quite easily be a curry base in its own right. If you are a lover of Southeast Asian flavours, this one will be right up your street.

SERVES 4 | PREP 5 MINS | COOK 10 MINS | BATCH

1 LARGE LEEK, THINLY SLICED

3 GARLIC CLOVES, FINELY CHOPPED

2 STICKS OF LEMON GRASS, BASHED

OLIVE OIL

2 TABLESPOONS RED CURRY PASTE

1 BUTTERNUT SQUASH, SKIN ON, DICED

1 X 400ML CAN OF COCONUT MILK (RESERVE 2 TABLESPOONS FOR GARNISH)

500ML VEGETABLE STOCK

SALT, TO TASTE

Sauté the leek, garlic and lemon grass in a pan in a little olive oil, along with a good pinch of salt, until the leek softens and the lemon grass becomes fragrant. Add the red curry paste and stir well.

Add the squash, the coconut milk and the stock and simmer for 10 minutes until the squash is soft enough to blend.

Fish out the lemon grass before transferring to a blender, or using a stick blender, and blending into a luscious fragrant soup.

Garnish with a swirl of coconut milk.

CHICKEN SOUP

OK, so I'm not sure I believe all the wondrous claims made about chicken soup, but it certainly packs a nutritional punch and is a great comforter, as well as being a brilliant way to use up any leftover roast chicken.

2 LARGE RED ONIONS, FINELY CHOPPED

3 GARLIC CLOVES, FINELY CHOPPED

3 CARROTS, FINELY DICED

1 THUMB-SIZED PIECE OF GINGER, PEELED AND SLICED

2 BAY LEAVES

OLIVE OIL

1 TEASPOON TURMERIC

1 LITRE CHICKEN STOCK

200G PEAS (FRESH OR FROZEN)

300G LEFTOVER ROAST CHICKEN, CHOPPED

In a pan, sauté the onions, garlic, carrots, ginger and bay leaves in a little olive oil, along with a good pinch of salt, for about 10 minutes. Remove the bay leaves, then stir in the turmeric.

Add the stock then simmer for another 10 minutes.

Remove about one third of the vegetables with a slotted spoon, ensuring you leave all the liquid, and set the veg aside.

Blend the remaining soup with a stick blender. Add the veg back in, along with the peas and the chicken, and simmer for another 5 minutes before serving.

TIP Beware of added salt and additives in shop-bought soups. Sometimes a seemingly healthy option is far from it. Chains can charge 4 times what it costs to make home-made soup and many have more than your recommended daily salt intake.

CARROT AND FENNEL

This fragrant, light soup is so simple and flavoursome. It can also be made into a delicious thick purée which tastes amazing with roast pork. To make this, simply use half the stock.

SERVES 4 · PREP 5 MINS · COOK 20 MINS · BATCH

1 LARGE RED ONION, FINELY CHOPPED

3 GARLIC CLOVES, FINELY CHOPPED

OLIVE OIL

600G CARROTS, DICED

2 FENNEL BULBS, ROUGHLY CHOPPED (SAVE THE FRONDS FOR SERVING)

1 SMALL POTATO, SKIN ON, DICED

1.5 LITRES VEGETABLE STOCK

SALT, TO TASTE

In a pan, sauté the onion and garlic in a little olive oil, along with a good pinch of salt, until the onion has softened.

Add the carrots, fennel and potato, and cover with the vegetable stock. Simmer for 10 minutes until all the vegetables are soft.

Transfer to a blender, or use a stick blender, and blitz until smooth.

Top with the reserved fennel fronds just before serving.

ROASTED CELERIAC

This soup is a great faff-free option. Just a couple of easy steps that allow you to get on with other things while it's cooking.

SERVES 4 · PREP 5 MINS · COOK 40 MINS · BATCH

2 CELERIAC, SKIN ON, DICED

OLIVE OIL

2 LARGE RED ONIONS, CUT INTO WEDGES

1.5 LITRES HOT VEGETABLE STOCK

SALT, TO TASTE

Preheat the oven to 180°C, 160°C Fan, Gas Mark 4.

Place the diced celeriac in a large roasting tin with a drizzle of olive oil and a pinch of salt. Place in the oven for 15 minutes before removing and adding the onions. Toss everything together well and return to the oven for another 20–25 minutes, stirring occasionally. The vegetables should be soft and turning a golden brown colour.

Transfer the roasted vegetables to a saucepan, along with the juices from the roasting tin – that's where all the amazing flavours are. Cover with the vegetable stock and blend, using a stick blender. Alternatively, transfer the roasted veg, juices and stock to a blender and blitz until smooth.

SOMETHING SWEET

CHAPTER
6

TIPS TO GET THE MOST OUT OF *EAT, SHOP, SAVE...*

I suggest that you follow the *Eat, Shop, Save* advice in this book for 8 weeks to really see how much of a difference you can make to how you feel – and to your bank balance! I want you to get as much out of the 8 weeks as possible, so here are some final tips to ensure that you do:

KEEP ALL OF YOUR RECEIPTS

So that you're able to calculate how much money you've saved at the end of the 8 weeks, you'll need to keep track of your spending. You could always take photos of your receipts and save them in a folder on your phone or computer so that you don't have bits of paper flying everywhere! There are many finance apps that allow you to scan in your receipts, which can help you track and manage your spending and budget.

And remember...
...always check your receipts! Make sure all your items were entered correctly and you received the advertised discounts. If you check your receipt before you leave the shop, it's much easier to ask about any discrepancies while you're still there. Plus, you might feel that it's not worth it once you're back home!

Keeping your receipts is also a good way to check any impulse buys that might creep in, even if you do have a shopping list. We often buy something we do not need or that isn't within our budget because of the appealing packaging, the fact that it's on sale and other environmental and sensory stimuli. We can do this even without thinking. Looking at your receipts can help identify where you might slip up with your spending and where you can improve on your savings. Even better, if you look at your receipt before you leave the shop, you get a chance to change your mind there and then and easily return what you don't actually need.

TAKE FOOD PHOTOS

Taking pictures of your meals is a great way to keep track of everything that you're eating and drinking. Photos of your food are the best way to see what portion sizes you are eating too.

TALK TO YOUR FAMILY AND FRIENDS

Especially if you have any breakthroughs (e.g. a really cheap shopping trip or a recipe that everyone loves!), or hit any challenges (e.g. struggling to break old habits). Discuss what is working and what isn't working so you can provide advice and support to each other throughout.

EXERCISE UPDATES!

Keep documenting any exercise you do, so everyone around you knows how you are getting on.

CHECK YOUR PROGRESS

If you'd like to test your progress with your weight loss or fitness then you could check what your weight and resting heart rate are each week, and let your family know the results. You can check your resting heat rate using a heart rate monitor and it's best to do this first thing in the morning, right after you wake up.

DETERMINATION!

The next 8 weeks will hopefully introduce you to simple changes that will enable you to lead a healthier, happier lifestyle – and ones that will stay with you for years to come. Ultimately, the more you put into it, the more you will get out of it. I am rooting for you!

FRUITY CHEESECAKE POTS

These cheesecake-like treats deliver all the right textures and flavours. The creaminess, the crunch, it's all there. This recipe contains the core elements of a classic cheesecake, just makes it a little bit healthier. The main reason these are so much better for you is because the sugar isn't there. You won't miss it – oatcakes are basically oat cookies without the sugar added. These pots are a great source of fibre and B vitamins.

SERVES 4 · PREP 30 MINS · CHILL 4 HOURS

100G OATCAKES

2 TEASPOONS BUTTER

½ TEASPOON CINNAMON

250G FULL-FAT SOFT CHEESE

250G BLUEBERRIES

250G STRAWBERRIES

Place the oatcakes between two tea towels and wallop them with a rolling pin, or any other suitable blunt instrument, to create crumbs.

Place the butter in a saucepan and melt over a low heat. Add the oatcake crumbs and the cinnamon and mix well until all the crumbs are coated with butter.

Using individual ramekins or tumbler glasses (one short enough and wide enough to get a dessertspoon into), add a 1.5cm layer of the buttered oatcake crumbs to the bottom and press down to form a base. Place the ramekins/glasses in the fridge to chill for 10 minutes.

Remove the ramekins/glasses from the fridge. Divide the soft cheese equally between the individual pots. Top with the blueberries and strawberries.

Return the pots to the fridge and chill for at least 4 hours.

STEVE'S STICKY BARS

In series one of the show, we met Steve who was a keen snacker and found himself reaching for high-sugar options that were affecting his health. So I created this gorgeous oat bar with a sticky texture and a lingering sweetness. The fibre in the oats will ensure a more gradual release of energy as well as being high in B vitamins for more sustained energy levels.

MAKES 16 SLICES

PREP 5 MINS

COOK 30 MINS

250G DATES, PITTED AND ROUGHLY CHOPPED

150ML WATER

2 TABLESPOONS PEANUT BUTTER

2 TABLESPOONS MIXED SEEDS

PORRIDGE OATS (NO SET WEIGHT, SEE METHOD)

Preheat the oven to 180°C, 160°C Fan, Gas Mark 4.

Place the chopped dates and water in a saucepan and simmer over a high heat until the dates start to break down to a mush.

Add the peanut butter and mix well to form a sweet nutty paste.

Add the seeds then add the oats in small increments, stirring constantly, until a stiff mixture has formed. You need the mixture to be sticky yet workable. The amount of oats you will need to achieve this will vary, hence no set measurement.

Place the mixture in a baking tin and press down well. Bake for 15–20 minutes, until golden brown on top.

Allow to cool fully before cutting into squares.

REPLACE AND SAVE
Replace shop-bought snacks with homemade ones and your savings will soon start adding up. Steve's Sticky Bars (see page 175) are a perfect pre- or post-workout snack.
Average cost = 40p
Average cost of a shop-bought protein bar = £1

Total Saving – 60p per snack

DATE AND ALMOND BALLS

The health world has gone energy-ball crazy, and I have seen all
sorts of weird and wonderful recipes using many strange ingredients.
This simple starter recipe is a great one and these really do make
a nice mid-afternoon snack. Sweet, but good for you.

MAKES **24** BALLS

PREP **5** MINS

COOK **0** MINS

250G PITTED DATES

250G WHOLE ALMONDS

2 TEASPOONS COCOA POWDER

This is the simplest method imaginable. Place all
the ingredients into a food processor and blitz on high
power until a dough has formed. It doesn't need to be
completely smooth, some texture is fine.

Break off pieces of the dough and roll into balls
about 2–3cm in diameter.

REPLACE AND SAVE
Average cost of Dale's Date and Almond energy ball x 8 = £6
Average cost of branded energy ball x 8 = £16

Total Family Saving: £10

BERRY YOGURT LOLLIES

**These are a snap to make and are a great treat on a hot day.
Fun, flavoursome and full of the good stuff.**

MAKES 8 LOLLIES
PREP 5 MINS
FREEZE 4 HOURS

150G BLUEBERRIES

150G BLACKBERRIES

250G PLAIN NATURAL YOGURT

2 TEASPOONS HONEY

Place all the ingredients into a food processor or blender and blitz into a smoothie-like mixture.

Pour the mixture into ice lolly moulds and place in the freezer for 4 hours or until solid. Simple as that!

TIP Supermarket yogurt, puddings, ice cream and ice lollies can be cheap, but beware of added sugar content. Luxury products tend to have even more sugar – up to 15g per portion.

CHOCOLATE ORANGE AVOCADO POTS

OK, you might think I have gone stark raving mad. But chocolate and avocado are now becoming a regular combination and these chocolate pots have taken the health world by storm. The avocado essentially works as a carrier for the flavour. It allows you to get the texture of a chocolate mousse or a ganache, but without the heavy ingredients. Give this a try and I guarantee you will be pleasantly surprised.

SERVES 4

PREP 10 MINS

CHILL 4 HOURS

2 VERY RIPE AVOCADOS, HALVED AND PITTED

ZEST AND JUICE OF 1 LARGE ORANGE

1 TABLESPOON HONEY, OR TO TASTE

3 TABLESPOONS COCOA POWDER

Scoop out the flesh from the avocados and place it in a food processor.

Add the remaining ingredients and blend into a thick chocolate orange mousse-like dessert.

Avocados can vary greatly in flavour. Some can have a mild, mellow flavour, others can be a little more bitter. So at this stage taste the dessert. You can add more cocoa powder to make it more chocolaty or more honey to make it sweeter.

Transfer the mixture into pots and chill in the fridge for 3–4 hours to firm up.

OATY BANANA BREAD

This is a cross between banana bread and a flapjack. Lovely stuff.

MAKES **10** SLICES · PREP **10** MINS · COOK **30** MINS

6 VERY RIPE BANANAS
(SKINS TURNING BROWN)

2 TABLESPOONS BUTTER

4 TABLESPOONS CRUNCHY
PEANUT BUTTER

2 TABLESPOONS HONEY

500G PORRIDGE OATS

60G WHOLEMEAL FLOUR

2 TABLESPOONS PUMPKIN SEEDS

Preheat the oven to 180°C, 160°C Fan, Gas Mark 4.

Peel the bananas and mash them with a fork. Keep a little bit of texture, they don't need to be super smooth.

Place the butter, peanut butter and honey in a saucepan and melt them together over a gentle heat. Mix thoroughly.

Add the mashed banana and mix well again. Then add the oats, flour and pumpkin seeds, and mix everything together thoroughly again until a gorgeous sticky mixture has formed.

Transfer the mixture to a shallow loaf tin and bake for 25–30 minutes, at which point the top should be golden. Insert a knife into the loaf. It should come out relatively clean, but this does have a gooey centre, which is part of its charm. If the knife comes out too sticky, give it another 8–10 minutes.

APPLE AND BLACKBERRY CRUMBLE

Who doesn't love a good fruit crumble? And you CAN make it healthy. There is no reason at all for there to be vast amounts of sugar in this dish. There is enough natural sweetness in the fruit to give you a delicious flavour.

SERVES 4

PREP 5 MINS

COOK 40 MINS

500G APPLES, CORED AND CUT INTO 1CM CUBES

250G BLACKBERRIES

FOR THE TOPPING

50G WHOLEMEAL FLOUR

75G PORRIDGE OATS

1 TEASPOON GROUND CINNAMON

Preheat the oven to 180°C, 160°C Fan, Gas Mark 4.

Place the chopped apples and the blackberries in a saucepan, and add a small amount of water – around 100ml. Simmer over a high heat for 10 minutes until the fruit cooks down and forms a jam-like mixture. Allow to cool slightly and the natural pectin in the apples and the sugar in both fruits will cause the mixture to thicken.

Place the fruit in a baking dish. Mix the topping ingredients together in a bowl and then sprinkle over the fruit.

Place the dish in the oven and bake for 25–30 minutes, until the topping is golden brown.

NO BAKE CAKES

OK, so these aren't cakes as such. They are cake-like, sticky bar-like, snack-like…however you want to describe them. But, they are perfect for when you get that desire for cake with a cuppa.

MAKES **6** SLICES PREP **10** MINS CHILL **8** HOURS

5 TABLESPOONS RAW MIXED NUTS (NOT THE ROASTED SALTED KIND)

4 TABLESPOONS MIXED SEEDS

2 HANDFULS OF DATES, PITTED

2 HANDFULS OF GOJI BERRIES OR RAISINS

4 TABLESPOONS COCOA POWDER

1 TEASPOON DESICCATED COCONUT

3 TABLESPOONS COCONUT OIL OR OLIVE OIL

Place all the ingredients except the oil in a food processor and blitz into a coarse mixture. It may take a little time for the different ingredients to break down, but you don't need to end up with a fine mix. The only thing necessary is that everything sticks together and will make a firm dough that holds its form.

Place the coconut oil, if using, in a saucepan and melt over a gentle heat. Once melted, pour it or the olive oil into the food processor with the other ingredients and blend again, making sure the oil has been mixed through the dough.

Transfer the dough to a square tin and press down firmly, pushing it right to the edge. Place in the fridge overnight, or for about 8 hours, before cutting into slices.

REPLACE AND SAVE
These quick and easy No Bake Cakes are healthy, nutritious and keep temptation at bay.
Average fat content in a slice of cake = 15g
Average fat content in a No Bake Cake bar = 7g

Total Fat Content Saving: 8g

MEAL PLANNERS

Here are some sample meal planners, using recipes from the book, to help you plan a week of evening meals. To make it even easier, I've included a list of all the ingredients you'll need. Each list is enough for four people for that week, so feel free to adapt it to your needs. Before you start, I suggest you make a few batches of the Hidden Veg Tomato Sauce on page 112 as quite a few recipes in these planners call for it. Making the sauce in advance will mean you'll find the recipes super quick. The lists of foods don't include the ingredients for the sauce.

WEEK 1

MONDAY
QUESADILLAS
PAGE 74

I absolutely adore quesadillas. They tick all the right boxes – delicious, comforting, easy and good for you. Winner! This dish calls for refried beans, which can easily be found in any supermarket.

TUESDAY
CHICKEN TRAY BAKE
PAGE 138

Tray bakes have become popular over the last few years, with many of those bake-in-the-bag packet mixes appearing on the market. This is the same principle but I guarantee it tastes a million times better.

WEDNESDAY
FRUITY FISH FAJITAS
PAGE 90

Fish is definitely something we should be eating more of. Cod can be quite expensive now, but another white fish has popped up that is cheaper and more sustainable – basa.

THURSDAY
MIXED BEAN CHILLI
PAGE 64

I do enjoy a good chilli. I love the meat variety and I love vegetarian versions too, and this mixed bean one won't disappoint.

FRIDAY
VEGGIE FRIED NOODLES
PAGE 118

Who doesn't love noodles? Just look at the queues at the well-known noodle outlets on a weekend and you can see that families love 'em! It is insanely simple to make this type of dish at home and you can load it up with all sorts.

WEEK 1 SHOPPING LIST

FRESH
4 WHITE FISH FILLETS, SUCH AS COD OR BASA

4 CHICKEN LEGS

4 CHICKEN BREASTS

2 LARGE EGGS

1 X 125G BALL OF MOZZARELLA CHEESE

8 TABLESPOONS GRATED CHEDDAR CHEESE

5 LARGE RED ONIONS

7 GARLIC CLOVES

4½ RED PEPPERS

1 GREEN PEPPER

1 COURGETTE

100G CHESTNUT MUSHROOMS

4 HANDFULS OF BABY SPINACH

1 RED CHILLI

4 SPRING ONIONS

1 RIPE MANGO

CUPBOARD
OLIVE OIL

2 TABLESPOONS BALSAMIC VINEGAR

2 TABLESPOONS SOY SAUCE

1 TABLESPOON SESAME OIL

300G NOODLES (UDON, EGG NOODLES, ETC.)

16 SOFT FLOUR TORTILLAS

6 TABLESPOONS REFRIED BEANS

2 X 400G CANS OF MIXED BEANS

2 X 400G CANS OF CHOPPED TOMATOES

2 TABLESPOONS BLACK OLIVES

20–30 JALAPEÑO SLICES (OPTIONAL)

2 TEASPOONS DRIED MIXED HERBS

2 TEASPOONS MEXICAN SEASONING

2 TABLESPOONS GROUND CUMIN

2 HEAPED TEASPOONS SMOKED PAPRIKA

SALT AND PEPPER

SERVING SUGGESTIONS
THURSDAY: BROWN RICE

WEEK 2
SHOPPING LIST

FRESH

8 CHICKEN BREASTS

8 SAUSAGES

200G FETA CHEESE

225G HALLOUMI CHEESE

4½ RED ONIONS

12 GARLIC CLOVES

1 GREEN CHILLI

2 RED PEPPERS

24–30 CHERRY TOMATOES

8 HANDFULS OF BABY SPINACH

2 HANDFULS OF MIXED SALAD LEAVES

2 SWEET POTATOES

1 LEMON

2–3 ROSEMARY SPRIGS

BUNCH OF FRESH MINT LEAVES

4 STICKS OF LEMON GRASS

CUPBOARD

OLIVE OIL

4 LARGE WHOLEMEAL PITTA BREAD

1 X 400G CAN OF CHICKPEAS

1 X 400G CAN OF CANNELLINI BEANS

4 X 400ML CANS OF COCONUT MILK

400G TOMATO PASSATA

8–12 TEASPOONS TOMATO PURÉE

16 BLACK OLIVES

2 HEAPED TABLESPOONS PEANUT BUTTER

600–750ML VEGETABLE STOCK

1 TEASPOON SMOKED PAPRIKA

2 TEASPOONS DRIED MIXED HERBS

1 TEASPOON TURMERIC

SALT AND PEPPER

SERVING SUGGESTIONS

TUESDAY: COOKED GREENS OR SALAD

THURSDAY: SWEET POTATO MASH

WEEK 2

MONDAY
CHICKEN AND HALLOUMI KEBABS WITH WHITE BEAN SALAD
PAGE 93

This dish calls for one of those store cupboard staples that can be a real life saver – tinned beans. They are such a great thing to stock up on as in a matter of minutes you can throw together a delicious meal with minimal effort. Wooden kebab skewers can be found in your supermarket.

TUESDAY
ROASTED SWEET POTATO, COCONUT AND WHITE BEAN SOUP
PAGE 155

This is such a delicious soup. Smooth, rich, flavoursome and incredibly nutrient dense. Slow-release carbohydrates, healthy fats, fibre, protein…Who'd have thought something so simple could be such a powerhouse.

WEDNESDAY
NUTTY LEMON GRASS CHICKEN
PAGE 82

This delicious dish, packed with glorious Southeast Asian flavours, is a true crowd-pleaser.

THURSDAY
SAUSAGE AND CHICKPEA HOTPOT
PAGE 142

This takes the classic sausage casserole and turns it on its head. Including chickpeas hugely ramps up the fibre and the B vitamins.

FRIDAY
PITTA PIZZAS
PAGE 129

This simple dish is an amazing hack. So many families spend a fortune on takeaway pizzas. And let's not fool ourselves, most of the takeaway pizzas around tend to be incredibly unhealthy – massively high in nasty fats and refined carbohydrates, and the calories per serving will make the mind boggle. This version will save you all that bad stuff, save you a heap of money and will give you a nutrient boost. Bargain!

WEEK 3

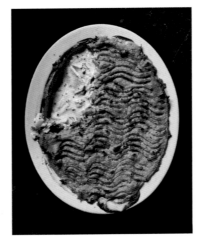

MONDAY
KALE AND MUSHROOM STIR-FRIED RICE
PAGE 89

This is a great all-in-one dish that will fill you up with the good stuff and is light and easy to cook. This calls for a packet of pre-cooked brown rice, a great ingredient to keep in your store cupboard.

TUESDAY
BEST FISH PIE EVER
PAGE 135

Fish pie is another of those absolute feel-good home favourites. Flavoursome, hearty, creamy. What's not to love? Well, the traditional one based on a roux can be incredibly rich and contain a lot of refined carbohydrates. This version is lighter and much more nutrient dense.

WEDNESDAY
SPANISH CHICKEN
PAGE 86

This simple dish is one that I predict will become a favourite in many households. It is absolutely gorgeous, and the flavours...wow! It's also a chance to get your hands a bit mucky and have some fun in the kitchen. Everything cooks together in one roasting tin too so minimal fuss.

THURSDAY
HONEY AND FIVE-SPICE PORK CHOPS
PAGE 98

These chops take minimal effort to prepare and cook but the end result is delicious. Pork goes so well with these flavours – a match made in heaven.

FRIDAY
TUNA PASTA BAKE
PAGE 144

This glorious dish is one of those crowd-pleasers that kids, fussy eaters and comfort-food lovers all unite on. This version takes this delicious classic and ramps it up nutritionally without even remotely skimping on taste. You can add additional veg if you like. I often add a couple of extra handfuls of spinach to the sauce and wilt it down. But don't worry if not, as it already has plenty.

WEEK 3 SHOPPING LIST

FRESH

800G FISH PIE MIX

4 CHICKEN LEGS

4 PORK CHOPS

100G EXTRA MATURE CHEDDAR CHEESE

3 RED ONIONS

2 WHITE ONIONS

7 GARLIC CLOVES

180G CURLY KALE

100G CHESTNUT MUSHROOMS

6 LARGE SWEET POTATOES

2 RED PEPPERS

20G DILL

2 ROSEMARY SPRIGS

500G LOW-FAT SOFT CHEESE

CUPBOARD

OLIVE OIL

1 X 250G PACKET PRE-COOKED BROWN RICE

300G WHOLEWHEAT PASTA

170G TINNED TUNA

400ML VEGETABLE STOCK

2 TABLESPOONS HONEY

1 TABLESPOON PEANUT BUTTER

6 TEASPOONS SOY SAUCE

5 TEASPOONS WHOLEGRAIN MUSTARD

2 TEASPOONS SESAME OIL

4 TEASPOONS CURRY POWDER

2½ TEASPOONS SMOKED PAPRIKA

1 TEASPOON CHINESE FIVE-SPICE POWDER

½ TEASPOON GARLIC POWDER

SALT AND PEPPER

SERVING SUGGESTIONS

TUESDAY: COOKED GREENS OR SALAD

WEDNESDAY: SALAD

THURSDAY: BROWN RICE AND SALAD

FRIDAY: SALAD

WEEK 4 SHOPPING LIST

FRESH

500G LEAN MINCED BEEF
8 CHICKEN BREASTS
1 TABLESPOON GRATED PARMESAN CHEESE
2 LARGE SWEET POTATOES
1 LARGE POTATO
3 RED ONIONS
1 LARGE WHITE ONION
13 GARLIC CLOVES

CUPBOARD

OLIVE OIL
800G TOMATO PASSATA
100G TIKKA MASALA PASTE
2 X 400G CANS OF BLACK BEANS
2 X 400G CANS OF CANNELLINI BEANS
1 X 400ML CAN OF COCONUT MILK
750ML VEGETABLE STOCK
+ 2 TEASPOONS STOCK POWDER
1 TEASPOON GROUND CUMIN
1 TEASPOON GROUND CORIANDER
1 TEASPOON MIXED FRESH HERBS
1 CINNAMON STICK
1 STAR ANISE
SALT AND PEPPER

SERVING SUGGESTIONS

MONDAY: COOKED GREENS OR A SALAD
TUESDAY: SALAD
WEDNESDAY: COOKED GREENS OR SALAD
THURSDAY: BROWN RICE
FRIDAY: BROWN RICE

NOTE: THE INGREDIENTS FOR THURSDAY'S BURGERS AREN'T INCLUDED HERE AS YOU HAVE A CHOICE! SEE PAGE 124 FOR WHAT TO INCLUDE IN YOUR SHOPPING LIST.

WEEK 4

MONDAY
SWEET POTATO COTTAGE PIE
PAGE 126

Cottage pie is one of those family staples that pleases every generation. Hearty, homely and warming, it has the ultimate feel-good factor. This version takes the classic comfort food and gives it a nutritional upgrade for good measure. Simple changes with big benefits.

TUESDAY
BLACK BEAN SOUP
PAGE 160

Ohhh this soup! There is something so comforting about it. Black beans have become really quite popular lately, and with good reason I say. They are very rich in a group of compounds called anthocyanins, which are responsible for their dark purple (not black at all, as it goes) colour pigment. These compounds are also found in red wine. They benefit heart health in several ways.

WEDNESDAY
CREAMY CHICKEN SPEEDY STEW
PAGE 100

Another insanely easy dish that's so moreish it's unbelievable. It's a one-pot wonder too, which is always good for days when you want to eat fast but eat well.

THURSDAY
BURGERS TWO WAYS
PAGE 124

Burgers are often seen as super unhealthy. This really needn't be the case though. When you make them yourself you can control what's in them, and actually they are just minced meat with whatever flavours you add. Simple, wholesome food. Here are two versions for some variety.

FRIDAY
CHICKEN TIKKA MASALA
PAGE 130

One of Britain's favourite dishes! A takeaway chicken tikka masala is a tasty treat for sure, but if you want a healthy *and* tasty version, this is it.

WEEK 5

MONDAY
**PIMPED-UP
LASAGNE**
PAGE 115

Now, this is family comfort
food at the highest level. Few
things beat a good lasagne.
This version really hits the
spot – and it has a nutritional
boost. We use the Hidden
Veg Tomato Sauce here, and
adding lentils to the mix
gives extra fibre, protein
and B vitamins.

TUESDAY
**TOMATO AND RED
PEPPER SOUP**
PAGE 156

This is one of the easiest
soups you could ever
imagine. Plus, it's packed
with antioxidants,
vitamin C, beta-carotene
and a whole host of
other goodies.

WEDNESDAY
TURKEY MEATBALLS
PAGE 107

These are a great thing to
stockpile the freezer with.
You can make boxes of them
and simply take a few out
to add to pasta, have with
a salad, or even have in a
sandwich – yep, really!
Super easy and delicious.
They can be shaped into
burgers too that are great
for the barbecue.

THURSDAY
SPINACH AND SWEET POTATO CURRY
PAGE 136

This dish is a true winner. It is a great beginner curry – one for people that have never cooked a curry from scratch and feel a little nervous about doing so. This proved a popular hit after I showed it on *Eat, Shop, Save* to Ellouise and Jamie, who stockpiled their freezer with this gorgeous dish. You can add prawns or other seafood at the end if you like to make different varieties.

FRIDAY
FISH FINGERS AND CHIPS
PAGE 121

There is no denying that fish fingers and chips is a family teatime institution. This version greatly boosts your omega-3 fatty acid intake and gives you a healthy dose of the antioxidant beta-carotene and fibre too!

FRESH

500G LEAN MINCED BEEF

500G TURKEY MINCE

4 SKINLESS SALMON FILLETS

50G SOFT CHEESE

SPRINKLE OF GRATED MATURE CHEDDAR

2 EGGS

4 RED ONIONS

6 SWEET POTATOES

2 LARGE HANDFULS OF BABY SPINACH

1 LARGE HANDFUL OF FRESH CORIANDER

7 GARLIC CLOVES

1 TEASPOON GRATED FRESH ROOT GINGER

2 GREEN CHILLIES

2 LARGE RED PEPPERS

CUPBOARD

OLIVE OIL

250G LASAGNE SHEETS

180G DRY RED LENTILS

OATMEAL

1 X 400G CAN OF CHOPPED TOMATOES

10 SUN-DRIED TOMATOES

1.3 LITRES VEGETABLE STOCK

¼ TEASPOON NUTMEG

2 TEASPOONS DRIED MIXED HERBS

1 TEASPOON GROUND CORIANDER

1 TEASPOON GROUND CUMIN

1 TEASPOON BLACK MUSTARD SEEDS

I HEAPED TEASPOON TURMERIC

SALT AND PEPPER

SERVING SUGGESTIONS

MONDAY: SALAD

TUESDAY: SALAD OR MIXED VEG

WEDNESDAY: HIDDEN VEG TOMATO SAUCE AND SALAD

FRIDAY: PEAS OR COOKED GREENS

WEEK 6 SHOPPING LIST

FRESH

4 CHICKEN BREASTS

200G SMOKED BACON LARDONS

300G LEAN MINCED BEEF

4 SIRLOIN STEAKS

8 TABLESPOONS GREEK YOGURT

520G FETA CHEESE

400G FROZEN PEAS

4 LARGE TOMATOES

2 SWEET POTATOES

4 RED ONIONS

7¬8 GARLIC CLOVES

3 GREEN CHILLIES

4 SPRIGS OF OREGANO

4 LARGE WHOLEMEAL PITTA

CUPBOARD

OLIVE OIL

300G WHOLEWHEAT PASTA

250G DRY RED LENTILS

4 X 400G CANS OF CHOPPED TOMATOES

1 X 400G CAN OF MIXED BEANS

40G SLICED BLACK OLIVES FROM A JAR

1 TABLESPOON RED WINE

1.2 LITRES VEGETABLE STOCK

200ML BEEF STOCK

1 TABLESPOON TOMATO PUREE

¼ TEASPOON TURMERIC

½ TEASPOON GROUND CORIANDER

1 TEASPOON GROUND CUMIN

1 TEASPOON SMOKED PAPRIKA

SALT AND PEPPER

SERVING SUGGESTIONS

TUESDAY: SALAD

WEDNESDAY: SALAD OR MIXED VEG

THURSDAY: BROWN RICE

WEEK 6

MONDAY
CHICKEN KEBAB
PAGE 67

When you have had a long day, the temptation to divert via the kebab house on your way home from work may be high. Once in a while is no problem at all, but getting into the regular habit of this can soon take its toll on your waistline and your wallet. This fresh, tasty version will scratch that itch, takes no effort at all and is a fraction of the cost.

TUESDAY
PASTA ARRABBIATA
PAGE 85

This gorgeous dish is pasta with a little kick. If there are people in the family who are sensitive souls when it comes to spice, then you can reduce the chilli or even leave it out. If not, go all in and see how lovely this dish is. Remember – always use wholewheat pasta for its higher fibre content.

WEDNESDAY
LENTIL AND BACON SOUP
PAGE 150

This is an absolute classic. OK, bacon may not be top of the healthy ingredients list, but a little bit now and again is all good. The lentils on the other hand...They are awesome. Rich in soluble fibre and protein, they keep you feeling satisfied, don't pack much in terms of calories and are a great source of B vitamins.

THURSDAY
CHILLI CON CARNE
PAGE 133

Chilli con carne isn't that unhealthy as dishes go, but some of the ready-made ones can have quite a high sugar content, which is why we were asked for a recipe for this family favourite. We also think every mealtime is an opportunity to get the good stuff in so of course we opted for the high-fibre upgrade – mixed beans.

FRIDAY
STEAK WITH PEA AND FETA MASH AND SWEET POTATO WEDGES
PAGE 76

This simple, speedy dinner is satisfying on so many levels.

WEEK 7

MONDAY
BOOSTED BOLOGNESE
PAGE 122

Spag bol. A real family favourite up and down the country – and one that can be a monumental calorie bomb if we aren't careful. This version created for the Smith family in the first series of the show went down an absolute storm. The changes aren't huge – just a couple of tweaks and this dish becomes so much better for you. By swapping white pasta for brown we up the fibre, and adding the lentils means extra protein, fibre and B vitamins.

TUESDAY
RED CURRY SQUASH SOUP
PAGE 163

This soup is serious! An absolute flavour explosion. This could quite easily be a curry base in its own right. If you are a lover of Southeast Asian flavours, this one will be right up your street.

WEDNESDAY
NORTH AFRICAN SPICED VEGETABLES, COUSCOUS AND HALLOUMI
PAGE 79

OK, so a mixture of Mediterranean elements here. But this dish is really simple, an absolute flavour bomb, and very nutrient dense and satisfying. A sure-fire favourite in the making.

THURSDAY
CROWD-PLEASING STIR-FRY
PAGE 141

Stir-fries often find themselves on the family favourites list but, I beg you, please stay away from the sugar-laden, over-processed, pre-made sauces. Learn how to create this simple staple from scratch. Building up these basic flavours will make a dish that tastes far superior, costs less and is much better for you. This recipe uses chicken but you can keep it veg, or swap the chicken for tofu, prawns or beef. All work beautifully with these flavours.

FRIDAY
ONE-POT CHICKEN CURRY
PAGE 104

This gorgeous dish is a double whammy – it's a perfect dish to batch cook and it's also a one-pot wonder so pretty hassle free. You can't get better. So, although this recipe serves 4, you can times it by as many as you like, depending on how many batches you want to make.

FRESH
500G LEAN MINCED BEEF

8 CHICKEN BREASTS

250G HALLOUMI CHEESE

5 RED ONIONS

17 GARLIC CLOVES

2 STICKS OF LEMON GRASS

1 LARGE LEEK

1 BUTTERNUT SQUASH

3 RED PEPPERS

1 YELLOW PEPPER

2 COURGETTES

1 SMALL AUBERGINE

150G CHESTNUT MUSHROOMS

250G GREENS

SMALL HANDFUL OF FRESH CORIANDER

CUPBOARD
OLIVE OIL

300G WHOLEWHEAT SPAGHETTI

250G COUSCOUS

680G DRY RED LENTILS

1 X 400ML CAN OF COCONUT MILK

2 X 400G CANS OF CHOPPED TOMATOES

1 TABLESPOON TOMATO PURÉE

400G TOMATO PASSATA

2 TABLESPOONS RED CURRY PASTE

4 TABLESPOONS MADRAS OR BALTI CURRY PASTE

250ML BEEF STOCK

1.8 LITRES VEGETABLE STOCK + 1 TEASPOON STOCK POWDER

2 TABLESPOONS SOY SAUCE

1 TABLESPOON TOASTED SESAME OIL

2 TEASPOONS HONEY

2 TEASPOONS CUMIN

1 TEASPOON SMOKED PAPRIKA

1 TEASPOON CHINESE FIVE-SPICE POWDER

1 TEASPOON CORNFLOUR

SALT AND PEPPER

SERVING SUGGESTIONS
MONDAY: MIXED LEAF SALAD

TUESDAY: SALAD OR VEG

THURSDAY: BROWN RICE

WEEK 8 SHOPPING LIST

FRESH

- 4 SALMON FILLETS
- 300G COOKED PEELED KING PRAWNS
- 4 SKINLESS CHICKEN BREASTS
- 200G MATURE CHEDDAR CHEESE
- 130G CHORIZO SAUSAGE
- 5 RED ONIONS
- 6 SWEET POTATOES
- 17 GARLIC CLOVES
- 4 GREEN CHILLIES
- 4-CM PIECE OF FRESH ROOT GINGER
- 1 SMALL BUTTERNUT SQUASH
- 3 LARGE COURGETTES
- 2 LARGE RED PEPPERS
- 1 ORANGE PEPPER
- 1 SMALL AUBERGINE
- OPTIONAL ADDITIONAL VEGETABLES (BABY SPINACH, PEAS, MUSHROOMS, ETC.)
- 2 HANDFULS OF BABY SPINACH
- 2 LIMES
- 2 HANDFULS OF FRESH CORIANDER

CUPBOARD

- OLIVE OIL
- 180G DRY RED LENTILS
- 1 X 400G CAN OF BUTTER BEANS
- 600G TOMATO PASSATA
- 1.1 LITRES VEGETABLE STOCK
- 8 TEASPOONS SOY SAUCE
- MILD CURRY POWDER
- 1 TEASPOON SMOKED PAPRIKA
- SALT AND PEPPER

SERVING SUGGESTIONS

WEDNESDAY: SALAD

THURSDAY: BROWN RICE

FRIDAY: BROWN RICE

WEEK 8

MONDAY
BUTTERNUT SQUASH, RED LENTIL AND WHITE BEAN STEW
PAGE 104

This is a wonderful dish for the colder months and freezes like a dream. Super simple and super cheap. It's also incredibly good for you, being high in fibre, B vitamins, antioxidants and protein.

TUESDAY
SALMON FOIL PARCELS WITH SWEET POTATO WEDGES
PAGE 80

This is one of the most faff-free recipes imaginable. Despite its simplicity, it is incredibly flavoursome, with plenty of complex carbs, protein, omega-3 fatty acids and fibre.

WEDNESDAY
GOOEY BAKED RATATOUILLE
PAGE 97

This is pure comfort food and tastes like heaven. Also, you'd struggle to find an easier dish.

THURSDAY
PRAWN AND CHORIZO MASH-UP
PAGE 94

This is a lovely flavoursome one-pan dish that is great for using up leftovers.

FRIDAY
FALLON'S CHICKEN CURRY
PAGE 116

In series one of the show, we created a curry that was a true crowd-pleaser and it highlighted perfectly how you can still enjoy your favourite dish, but by modifying the recipe you can create a far healthier version. Making the sauce with velvety sweet potato is a great technique for getting veg into fussy eaters.

INDEX